DON'T SNIFF THE GLUE:

A TEACHER'S MISADVENTURES IN EDUCATION REFORM

by:

DAWN CASEY-ROWE

Spread joy... Be awesome :) Dawn

Cover design by: Erin Tyler

Interior design by: Erin Tyler

Cover photograph by: Jodi Swanson

Cover model by: Jodi Swanson

Author Photograph by: Alison Casey

Library of Congress Control Number

2014915668

ISBN: 978-0-9906737-0-5 (E-books)

978-0-9906737-1-2 (Print)

FOR:

DECLAN

May you enjoy your education.
May it serve you well.

CONTENTS

FOREWORD

As educators we have bookcases, either in our class-rooms, behind our desks or somewhere in our homes, chock full of "teacher" books. Their glossy covers glisten on the shelves with the promise of making us better at our jobs. These publications offer insight on how to engage students, how to manage our classrooms, how to lead impactful profes-sional development, and so on.

I find those books to be the three Bs of reading—bland, beige and boring.

I have longed for a first-person education book told from the per-spective of teachers and students. I have always wanted to turn the pages of a "teacher" book that reads like a novel and makes me feel as if the author was writing right from my classroom.

Students staring at teachers with blank faces as teachers stand in the front of the room delivering initiatives they don't believe in—that they must because the state has commanded everyone to do so. Teachers talking over coffee about leaving the profession to do something epic—start a paddleboard biz in the Florida Keys, fold t-shirts at the GAP or even write a book about what really happens in education.

This is that book.

Dawn Casey-Rowe has written a beautiful first story about what it's like to be a teacher. She has captured the love, hate, comedy and tragedy of what it's like to believe in young people and try to provide them with an innovative experience within our pubic school system. Her style of writing is just enough wit, sarcasm and storytelling to hook the reader while providing prospective on a profession misunderstood by many.

–KATHLEEN JASPER,
CONVERSATIONED

1

ARE YOU SURE YOU WANT TO DO THIS?

I wake up each morning. I get dressed. I drink way too much coffee. On a lucky day, I catch a nice sunrise on my drive. I get out of the car, pack mule three or four bags up a five-mile ramp, nod good morning to the cluster of zombie-students who muster a smile. They're forced out of teen coma far too early—they try to miss the alarm but parents scream and make them get dressed.

I walk into the building. I check the mailbox for notices left rotting. All but two could have been better ignored in email form saving a rainforest, a spotted owl, or a Christmas tree or two.

I go to the sign-in sheet. I write my name, or something similar—

I wonder if it gets read. I talk to the office staff.

I head upstairs to drink even more coffee…

Two complainers dot the landscape, fixtures on the ramp. The time on the school clock is five hours ahead—must be set for school in Europe. Perhaps I am running late? I talk to a student who's as early as me. We smile.

The day begins…

FOR THE LOVE
OF THE GAME

P eople ask why I teach—it's a difficult time in education today. Sometimes, it's hard to say.

I love my students. I love looking into their faces, seeing their inner light, asking it to shine. I love telling them, "You can have a life you love. Here's how…" I love watching their postures change when they realize we're talking about secrets to life that are never going to be found in a textbook—real things that define success.

I love watching the kid who says, "I'm staying back," straighten up after I turn his "deficits" into some of his greatest superpowers. He's going to use them to fly into the stratosphere.

I love the subversiveness of discovering a student's goals and desires within a system that increasingly puts them—and me—in boxes. Boxes that are taped, categorized, stored, and labeled with test scores, letters, and evaluations determining our fates.

Teaching isn't something a person learns in a textbook or class, certainly not in this book. It's not something gathered from hundreds of pages of pedagogy in graduate school. It's a gift you get and give standing in front of thousands of kids—the ones who shine, and the ones who've been covered up for far too long. It's something you learn by giving all you have to those you serve—teaching them to be great, planting seeds that will flower years later.

The moment I get close to mastering teaching is the moment I realize students teach us—make us great—more than we do for them. Teaching is a lifetime of study.

It's a cycle of give and take, of convincing students to learn, marketing the fact that what I have to share is of value, then making sure it truly is—no different from building a business or pitching a product for "As Seen on TV."

"Here, I have lessons for success. Take them! Only three easy payments of $19.99. But WAIT, there's MORE! Buy now and receive a free guidebook on what to do when life kicks you around. Pay only shipping and handling."

Because life will kick them around even more than school, and I won't be standing next to them to cushion the blow—despite the fact I tell them I give a "lifetime guarantee."

I left Corporate America to teach over a decade ago. Teaching wasn't a controversial career then, and I wanted to save the world. In the course of my short 1.3 decades in the classroom, I've watched education crumble around me generating controversy I never would have imagined. Sadly, respect for public education has declined nationally. People grumble about teachers in the news and policymakers who've never stepped a foot in the classroom make decisions that affect my life and the lives of those I teach. Policies that require I be rated for engaging students disengage my kids with weeks of testing with tests that cause them to fear for their lives when graduation comes.

Those kids, my customers in essence, ask questions I can't answer, "Miss, why do we all have to learn the same thing?"

"Miss, why do we spend weeks of our time testing?"

"Miss, why isn't the textbook useful?"

"Miss, why didn't we learn any of this in school?"

I have no answers.

There's a certain feeling I get as an adult when a child or teen speaks the absolute truth. A truth so pure and undeniable I'm silenced—when they cut through the smoke, mirrors, and BS and show me my reflection. Our reflection. They do it often. A good teacher says, "You're right. Thank you." An insecure adult pushes back, bullies, puts the blame on the student. "If you just knew your math we wouldn't have to test you for seven weeks…"

We have a host of things to improve in education. There's nothing wrong with that. Learning is continual and lifelong. There's always something to teach, something to learn, opportunities for positive change. I want to do education reform correctly, though, so my son and students get the gift of learning that was given to me. It's the gift I treasure most from my own time in school.

I sit on the front lines, watching the media report how other countries beat me into the pavement and stomp on my test scores mocking me in seven languages. Maybe it's true, but I'll say this—we are making miracles with students every day in the space of seven hours, and now that technology permeates every corner of our universe, sometimes we're on stage 24/7. American education helps every single kid, regardless of income level, background, gender, religion, or special need. If you're a girl in America, you get an education. If your parents didn't graduate, you get an education. If you can't afford books or uniforms, you get an education. If you're a member of a minority religion, you get an education. If you're the child of a migrant worker, you get an education. If you learn differently, you get an education.

In a nation this size and diverse, that's incredible. And for that, I'll stand up to the press, pundits, and politicians any day of the week. Can we do better? Yes. This book is a series of stories and reflections—some things I've seen and experienced, and some I hope for. If I stay in teaching, maybe what I wish for will come true. If I move on, I hope by teaching, I leave the world a better place. I'll see my work continue through the paths of my students.

I want the teaching world to be better so when someone says, "I want to be a teacher," people congratulate them the same as if they said, "I want to be a doctor."

That didn't happen to me. If I tell people I teach, they say, "Oh, you're a teacher? I wouldn't want to do that." or "You're so over-qualified… why are you teaching?" When I introduce myself as a writer or business owner, they say, "That's awesome!"

It's a shame. Teaching is more important.

It's my dream that the nation will realize this very soon.

DAWN CASEY-ROWE

15

IN THE BEGINNING...

I teach to change the world.

I teach to make the next generation better than me.

I make them love what they do.

I give them tools to think on their own...

> To do great things

> To live lives better than mine.

In the middle...

I *need* them to pass the test.

I *need* them to graduate.

I *need* them to have all their credits.

I *need* to do this paperwork and adhere to policy.

In the end...

Tests don't matter. Only vision.

Whose vision? Theirs, not mine.

The goal... race into the stratosphere.

> Make them love what they do... see them do great things.
>
> Live life with joy. And know "best" isn't about money.
>
> Teach them to smile...because life's too short

> ...for anything less.

SITTING AT MY DESK

It's the beginning of the year, a typical day, learning combined with a touch of theatrics.

I sit at my desk and kick up my feet, tossing cashews high in the air, catching each in my mouth for show. My students complete a scavenger hunt introduced with five minutes of hard-core comedy. They're having fun. Maybe this class won't be as bad as they feared.

I memorized their names on Day One, which amazed them. They love the fact I said textbooks are dumb. Even the school-hater in the corner who thinks I can't see her texting has begun to smile.

I feel like a rock star. These are the best moments in teaching… the critical time when kids come out of their shells and peek around. They decide how the year's going to be and if they want to be a part of it.

This is how I imagined teaching would be. Teens leaning over desks discovering the meaning of life. Asking, "What do I do to become great?"

I wanted them to see they could pass me on the road of life and be better than me, and I'd be proud.

I wanted them to know there'd be someone in their corner any time they needed it. Life gets ugly—it throws punches until the last second of the last round. I'd tell them I'd be by the stool if they needed me waiting to make the cut so they could see through the blood and tears—get through that final round to the bell. I wanted them to know that.

But today, I sit at my desk tossing cashews, wondering which kids will dive off the high dive and get a perfect ten, which I'll have to tug along, and which will drown. It breaks my heart when the life rafts don't work. I've been teaching for a while. I know they won't all get to the finish line. But the ones that make it big are never the ones I'd bet on in Vegas. That, I know, too. It's why I never give up. Even when they do.

For now they watch me toss cashews. And they try to win the game.

Life is but a stage... Only they don't know we're playing for real.

I remember the day I decided to teach. I heard a voice in my cubical.

"You need to leave your job and teach." There are only two things to do when you start hearing voices. Go on extended vacation to a place with bad food, locks, and straight jackets, or assume the Almighty is trying to help and obey. I hoped the second was true. I applied to graduate school the next week.

My friend wasn't pleased.

"Are you *serious,* Casey? You're going to be a teacher? You're *so* overqualified for that." It was six years into my first career.

When I started that career, he'd said, "You're so overqualified for that..." too. I was floundering. What was I qualified for? Did he think I should run for President? Or Pope?

At one point I had an offer in hand to be a police officer.

"You wasted your degree if you're going to do that!" he said.

I wanted to save the world. Law enforcement seemed to fit the bill. Who doesn't love an Irish cop, even three generations removed?

My uncle was a police officer in Bridgeport, Connecticut. He'd never tell police stories, even when I worked in auto insurance and needed his help on a suspicious situation. He'd done some pretty big things as a police officer, then detective. He retired having made the city a better place. Silently.

One day when I was working in insurance, I picked up a Bridgeport police report. I needed it for my file. It was back in the days when I had to drive to the station, hand over four or five dollars, and request a hard copy of the report in person by smiling at the clerk. It had been over two decades since Uncle Jim retired. An old-timer sat behind the desk.

"Maybe you knew my Uncle Jim?" His face lit up. He started talking about the old days. Of course he knew my uncle—they'd worked together as beat cops. Everyone knew my Uncle Jim. It was how it was to be in law enforcement in those days. Community. Respect for the law and for the man. Family. They'd worked at a time when the neighborhood officer was an essential member of the city, a pillar. A rock, when kids causing mischief knew the police would lift them up by the scruff of the neck, bring them home, and parents would take care of the rest.

Twenty years after retirement, my uncle's work was alive on the streets.

I never understood why he wouldn't tell his stories. I guess being a police officer is a hard thing to do—he'd seen things he couldn't unsee, the darker side of life. Jobs like that aren't always about fixing things. It's more about keeping them at bay. Now that I've been around the block a few times myself, I see the irony—teaching's not much different.

I was about to accept my appointment to the police academy.

The phone rang. It was my uncle.

"Your father tells me you're going to be a police officer," he said. "This is no career for a girl." He was adamant, bordering on displeased.

He assured me there would be no world changing in the first years of my career, if ever. Law enforcement was a lot about maintaining the status quo. Putting out fires. Paperwork. Filing.

24

Stapling. Doing the mundane, hoping nothing hit the fan. Files? Reports? It sounded a lot like the work I was already doing.

Another family friend said, "Are you the kind of person who takes work home with you? Who feels personally bad for people? Who wants to make life better for everyone? This job will change you. Imagine sending a kid back to an abusive home because the judge won't write the order, or not being able to do what you know is right because of a statute? Can you do that over and over and not break down? Because things like that will be a normal part of your job."

He knew me. He was right. What he didn't know was many of those same things would be part of teaching. Ultimately, they would change me. I'd come to that precipice where I knew I'd given it all and still couldn't help that one kid desperately in need. The kid without documentation, whose mom had cancer, who couldn't buy school clothes, who wanted me to take her in. The kids who died.

I'd have to learn to come back from the cliff and find balance. To kill the savior complex. To realize, as a friend put it, that the "simple act of loving" is what changes the world, not actively fixing its ills.

I declined my appointment to the police academy. I felt like I was backing down though. When it was time to pull the trigger, I always put the safety back on.

25

My colleague convinced me to apply to the FBI. It seemed like good fit for me. If being a beat cop meant I'd be giving tickets and filing reports, the FBI might be a place where I could really make a difference.

We had to be in top shape, so we went to the seedy gym every morning to lift and work out—the 4am spot where the drug dealers, gangsters, dancers, and Mafiosi went for a quick workout after a tough night. I liked these people, even though they'd be the ones we'd have to take off the streets. We all spotted each other for reps on the taped up weight benches and talked about Yankee games. They seemed like good people—just in different lines of work.

My friend got accepted to the Academy. I put the safety back on the trigger again. I should have gone, too. I was in a relationship. Someone I cared about—thought I might even grow to love— "hated Feds." I backed down again. Maybe, I thought, the FBI wasn't for me.

"Are you crazy?" I'd have told my twenty-something self. "Don't listen!" I'd have kicked myself, "Go, be awesome. You have talent." I'd have said people close to me should encourage me, not make me feel my dreams are stupid or wrong. People speak from their own bias—their self-interest, and I should refuse to be put in their boxes. More importantly, I should release myself from my own.

I think of these stories today. The mistakes I've made are opportunities if I flip them upside-down. They're things I teach my students. If I teach them nothing else, it's this: make your own decisions. Be great because you believe in yourself. Don't be stifled… Don't put the safety back on the gun.

I wonder if my twenty-something self would've listened. I wonder if she would've been on the road to great much sooner?

Or maybe she'd have graduated the Academy and been shot by some mobster on his way out of the seedy gym in search of a meatball sandwich.

It's best not to know.

My twenty-something self wouldn't have wanted to die over a meatball sandwich. She had something greater to live for. She just didn't know it yet.

SHAKESPEARE'S NOT FOR ME

I didn't teach right out of school. I got a regular job. It didn't take long to get into the patterns of life and lose interest in them. How was going to work every day looking at files saving the world?

I was a typical over-impressionable twenty-something, half a decade into a career that felt like a thirty-year sentence. It's what most people feel after graduation, "What's next?" I couldn't focus on an insurance career forever. I wasn't sure I had the stomach for it. Or the attention span.

I had my crowd of happy hour friends. We went to concerts, football games, parties, and picnics. The next day, we returned to work on the same stuff with different names on the files. My heart wasn't in it. I never filed efficiently. I didn't staple right, clean my desk, or document the notes. "Attention to detail," they'd say. I drove my boss crazy with big ideas. My job wasn't to have big ideas. It was to document files. I was bored. Replaceable.

The part I loved was helping people. I held their hand and walked them through the resolution of car accident claims. Whether I had good news or bad, we connected. They appreciated my help. To those people, I mattered.

That was the feeling I cherished. It was the lesson I took with me from that career—true empathy. Sometimes, people had a simple problem with a quick resolution. Other times, their lives were destroyed. I didn't want them to feel like paperwork.

I ached for these people. People whose policies had lapsed who'd be financially ruined by their accidents. People who had been hurt and disabled. An old lady, a mom of a murder victim, the man who's fiancé was paralyzed the week before their wedding when a tree fell across the road onto her car as she passed by. I did my best—even if only for a moment—to help those who my life touched in the slightest measure.

In insurance everything is translated into a number, from a hangnail to a human being. It's what the actuaries do. It's what I hated. I figured teaching would be the opposite. Much to my chagrin, I found the entire universe boils down to the numbers. They are the essence of human existence. I should've known—

it's what my math teachers told me in high school. I thought they were exaggerating because they were math teachers and they loved themselves, but it turns out, they were telling the truth. I couldn't escape math by changing careers, even if I was going to teach history. Even dead people in history books need to be accounted for somehow.

Teachers and students are translated into numbers, too. Test scores, evaluations, grades—there's no escaping it—everything in life boils down to the data, right down to the value of human life, something I learned in my first career. The actuaries can calculate the value of a life down to the penny by considering a person's role in life, earning potential, age, and other factors.

I often think, what is my value? The value of my students?

What is the value of a person in society?

And so I began teaching—a nerd with a strong desire to create the next generation of nerds. They'd all go to Yale and Harvard and think big things.

The reality was different. The kids didn't smile at every lesson and bring in their homework like the teaching book said.

"Nothing personal, Miss, I like you. Shakespeare's not for me." I wasn't even teaching Shakespeare. I teach history—stories about dead people across the globe, not literature—dead people who wrote big words. I didn't understand.

"Shakespeare's Not for Me" was about to be the teacher. All my degrees and the pile of books in my brain hadn't taught me to listen… to *really listen* to what students needed.

Listen—like I'd listened to people pour out their hearts about accidents for years.

I was giving students what I wanted them to have—what was important to me. I was failing to listen to their dreams, values, and plans.

There's a disconnect, sometimes, between the ideals of educators and the goals of students and families. The system tries to tell families what's best for their kids. It's presumptuous and degrading.

I was guilty.

You will all go to Yale and Harvard and get degrees in…

There's only one solution. Listen. I want students to listen—I must do the same. Listen to what's deep in their hearts. What are their hopes and dreams? How can I help? No one cares about anything I teach unless it serves them. I have to provide value— show how skills I teach will help them build their future. I must encourage dreams, not construct them. Hand kids the hammer and the saw, let them build.

There's always temptation to superimpose values upon students. Creating a "generation of scholars" was my dream, and not a particularly useful one at that.

"Shakespeare's Not for Me" had a family business. A towing company. Not only did he have a towing company, he had what he did not know was a solid business plan.

"I'm going to expand our towing contracts with police departments and buy more trucks to take over this area, too." I'd paid lots of tow bills working in insurance. This kid had everything he needed to make his dreams real—he didn't need a dime to do it. Shakespeare, he thought, was getting in his way. Dead bards should never interfere with the financial success of the living.

I asked him to give Shakespeare a chance. Sometimes things we learn now pop up later and help us when we don't expect it, or at the very least enrich our lives. That's been my experience, anyway. The things I learn today meet up with things I learned yesterday and eventually synthesize into something I never expected tomorrow. Something amazing.

He gave me a shot at teaching, and I helped him the best I could. We both learned from each other. Teaching should never be a one-way street. It's a relationship.

I came to teaching to change the world. In the process, I changed myself.

Sometimes I get discouraged. I wonder if I matter, if I'm still replaceable like I was in so many other jobs and careers, measured only by numbers.

I look down at a quote scrawled across a page. A friend wrote—quite simply—"You... are... magic." Sometimes I need magic. Other times I think I might be that magic. The thought keeps me going just a little while longer.

T wo years after I made the decision to teach, I finished all the required classes and jumped through the necessary hoops. I was hired.

"Here's your classroom."

This is the day every finally employed teacher dreams about. The world told me not to be a teacher. They said I'd "…never be hired—too much competition."

And then it happened. Someone proved them wrong and handed me the keys to a room in a building that would be filled with bright, eager minds.

A colleague walked me to the room. He was vacating it for a room in the new section of the school.

Room 222. My room. It was an odd color. Salmony-barf. I'd seen that color before. I couldn't place it. It tugged at my mind.

That color… the salmon on the wall… Where have I seen that color before?

Jail.

I'd done my time in jail. As a volunteer, not a guest. Salmony-barf was the color of Youth Max. The state must have gotten a massive sale on salmony-barf. There was no geographical region, modern style, or historical era that inspired that color. It was the color of Caucasian cadaver. And the color of Room 222. I was one of the lucky ones. Some of the rooms were an unpainted cell block gray.

On his way out, my colleague gifted me a very special piece of furniture.

"You'll love this," he said. I looked closely. It was a rustic, hand-crafted shelf of sorts. The slots were very close together, about forty in total, twenty on each side. It wasn't a bookshelf.

"It's a paper organizer. Copy your papers and put them here. I don't need it." That's what happens with teachers. At a certain point, we have too much stuff. We gift it to the next generation. Our trash becomes their gold and platinum.

"Don't mind that black mark on the heater," he said on his way out. "It caught fire. It should be okay now." I looked around. There was a teacher desk filled with old stickers, student desks with a lifetime supply of gum, and a little table in the front of the room. Room 222 was all mine. He left. I stood and marveled.

Just then, a lady wandered through the back door of the room without speaking, a specter in a movie. She did not say hi. She didn't introduce herself. She glided, six inches from my face, approaching the special shelf. She motioned toward it. The shelf levitated and floated toward the door.

"Um, hi." I said. "I'm Dawn. Nice to meet you."

The specter hovered, then drifted another few feet toward the door.

"I'm the new social studies teacher."

No response. She went a bit further. Should I speak?

"I'm sorry," I said, by way of introduction, "That's my shelf."

She stopped. She stared. After a moment her mouth opened and shut once or twice. Her arms rattled like the apparition of Jacob

Marley upon his first meeting with Ebenezer Scrooge, but her voice was soft and distant.

"No, it's mine…" she said, gazing at a fixed point far behind my head.

"Well, Mr. G. just brought me here and gave it to me. He said his students made it for him, but he doesn't need it anymore."

She stopped. She froze again. Defeated by facts, she rattled her chains silently. The shelf dropped from midair, crashing to the ground. She floated away.

Beginning a teaching career felt a bit like being a character in *The Twilight Zone*. The rules didn't make sense for career-changers like me. It was surreal—a "fend for yourself" mentality, the opposite of Corporate America, where supplies are neatly placed in closets next to an SOP manual explaining precisely what to do. Teaching was very different, never logical.

Getting what I needed wasn't simple like going to a cabinet and picking up a pencil to start the day. Requisitioning a pencil could take weeks and several pencils to accomplish. When we got supplies, we learned to hoard and hide them like Soviets under communist rule. Save everything. Trade for what you really need.

I learned to obey bells like one of Pavlov's dogs. Eating's done on cue in schools. Going to the bathroom is also done on cue.

Almost every function—be it academic or bodily—has a bell or a very short time slot associated with it. This was a very different concept from Corporate America, where we enjoyed the "lunch hour," and went to the bathroom whenever we wanted. A teacher's lunch is eighteen minutes. I can choose between eating or using the bathroom. I never finish eating. The kids, I noticed, don't either.

School ends at 2:11. Not 2:10 or 2:15. Everyone knows when the last bell rings. In business, a person's workday ends when the pile shrinks enough that going home is a good idea. In schools, it's precise. The bell rings, we go—a two-hundred-year-old habit taken from the New England factory system that dog trained us into shape.

Everything I did in schools required combatting logic and common sense. The floating ghost stealing furniture should have warned me I'd entered a career where the seemingly normal intersected with the bizarre. A career where I'd create a ponderous chain of red tape.

I've labored on it since.

My dream is that schools will take things we've accepted as status quo—scheduling, requisitioning, evaluating, and teaching, and look at creative ways to better serve students, families, educators, and educational leaders in that order.

That way, we can spend more time teaching and talking about the really big questions in life and less time getting over the hurdles.

FOR WANT OF A TAB

Even though the pundits say education's terrible and friends say, "Why do you want to do *that?*" a lot of people want to be teachers. It's a job that makes a difference. People *dream* of being teachers—I did. I'd line up stuffed animals, absolving my favorites of homework, putting the bad ones in the corner.

My high school teachers told me to be a teacher. I should've listened right away.

I read a quote about writing that's true for teaching as well. The quote says if friends read your work and say you should be a

writer, you should *not* be a writer. If friends who
tell you to write, then you should, because only a
understands the pain, suffering, and hard work o

Only another teacher knows the truth about teaching, the joys,
the heartbreak, the absolute need to save the universe. My teachers spotted something in me. I now see this in others. It's not
as simple as a desire to save the world—it's a desire to watch
people lift themselves up—to provide a guiding hand with a
smile. Done right, it's a combination of mentorship with the
absence of ego. When my students become bigger than me, I've
done my job. The best teachers hope for this.

I didn't teach right away, I wandered through life first, took a
few punches, and got a little lost.

I wonder what type of teacher I'd have been if it were my first
career. Probably a bland one. Teachers, like writers, need to have
some life under their belts to make it real. No one truly understands life at twenty. Or ever, really… but still, I had to have
something to show students first. I had to have lived. Only then
could I explain what it's like to live, and how to prevail when the
chips are down. No one really knows that at eighteen, twenty,
twenty-five. I'm glad I waited.

I had to be ready to teach.

Before any new teacher gets a class, however, he or she gets hazed, run through the gauntlet, tested in the crucible. Then The Machine decides who can teach. I've seen some terrible people get through the hoops, and one or two of the best get cut. The meat grinder is often very subjective and cruel toward people who would've brought immense light to the classroom had they been approved. Teacher prep programs can't know who's going to be the best teacher. Only students know that.

There should be a disclaimer for everyone applying to a teacher program:

"Thanks for cutting your salary and earning potential in half to change the world. Glad to have you. You'll eat ramen through grad school while you learn facts you'll never use. You'll mold yourself into someone else's textbook idea of how to wake kids and cram test facts into their heads. You'll spend two years role-playing outdated situations with peers. You'll take three exams naming dead educational philosophers, then you'll attempt a million multiple choice questions based on scenarios from 1920s Oklahoma. And you will say you'll never be tempted to Velcro a kid to his seat. Finally, there will be a lab practical in which you identify eighty types of craft glue by scent and physical proper-ties, cross-indexing for potential toxins. Oh yeah, and here's the amortization schedule for your student loan. You'll be paying past forty."

Don't sniff the glue!

Or lose your identity in the process.

New teachers are hazed. I was hazed. I took a million education classes, drove around the state doing observations and practice teaching, and finally completed two sections of student teaching. Most people did one, but I wanted to teach middle school. Midway through student teaching, I realized I'd been placed in one of two remaining "junior high schools" in the state.

Junior high schools and middle schools are not the same. Sure, they both house twelve-year olds, but junior highs, in theory, are old school. In my mind, a seventh grader trying to blow off homework in a junior high did it the same way as the kid in the middle school, but there are whole PhD theses full of pedagogy saying junior highs are different. Without the correct semantics, practicing in a school with a sign that said "middle school," I wouldn't be certified for that level. A kind soul from my graduate history program took me into his "middle school" class. Requirement done.

I was almost ready to earn my students.

The last thing I had to do to be rubber stamped was pass the technology test—an exam measuring whether I knew enough tech to stand in front of a classroom filled with twenty or thirty kids not permitted to use smartphones.

The test consisted of three parts. Type something, chuck something on a spreadsheet, and successfully send an email. It was the final circus hoop standing between my teaching certification and me.

I failed.

Impossible. I used technology in my corporate job about as much as commonly existed outside of tech fields. I couldn't imagine teaching required more than that. Most schools didn't provide the technology they were asking us to use anyway. Except for my teacher station, I wouldn't see a computer in my class for a decade.

Failed? Must be an error.

"Excuse me." I approached the proctor. "This is a mistake. Can you explain my results to me?"

"No," he said, "We're very busy. We just give scores."

Computer generated scores that determine the life course of a person? *Impossible!*

Not impossible. Reality—in and out of the classroom. I just didn't know it yet. Computerized, no-feedback tests determine whether many kids graduate these days.

"I'm sorry, I really need you to take a moment and explain this to me." This was important. My career was at stake.

"We can't. There are too many people. Not possible."

I looked around the room. It was empty. If there was a place to take a number, I didn't see it. I was the only failure in the room demanding help.

I'd lived in Russia for a short spell. In Russia, the art of defeating bureaucracy is a matter of life or death. I'd wait. This guy couldn't hold a candle to a post-Soviet bureaucrat.

"There's no one here. There is no way I failed this test. I need feedback so I can retake the test." It seemed terribly odd to retake a test without knowing what was wrong in the first place. The education program had entire courses dedicated to the importance of giving feedback to students.

"No." He was holding his ground. It was probably the only power he had in life, and I was on the receiving end of its misuse. He was a Rhode Island politician in training.

All of a sudden, I heard something I hadn't heard in a long while, my corporate voice. It was the opposite of the education voice I was developing. The education voice smiled and said things like "Good job," and "I know you'll do better next time!" The corporate voice had a smile behind it, too, but a very different one—a negotiation smile. When I see the negotiation smile I know someone's about to stick a knife in my back, and I have to outflank him to live. I smile back.

"Let me restate this so I understand, because I intend to quote you. This program—which trains teachers to give effective feedback—*refuses to give feedback to students on tests that affect their careers?* Perhaps I can retake this test by typing an email to the newspaper and copying the deans asking them to better explain this? May I have your name?"

I got my feedback without a smile. It turned out the computer program only read formatting. No human looked at the tests to see if the answers made sense. It all boiled down to typing. I learned to type long ago—an eighth grade teacher identified my interest in writing and tried to help me along the way.

"Use two spaces after the period and five to indent a paragraph." She was older, practicing proper secretarial conventions for her time. I went home and practiced on my cast-iron Royal typewriter, the model, I later discovered, used by Hemingway. I typed day and night. Two spaces after the period, and five to indent a paragraph. Backspace, shift, correct. Carriage return.

She was right—typing was one of the most valuable skills I learned. It would carry me through life into things I loved, but wouldn't get me past this bureaucrat-in-training on his high-stakes test.

The test required me to use the "tab" button to indent, not five-spaces hit manually, and it only permitted one space after the period. A tab and a space would have kept me from my teaching career.

That's the danger in standardized tests these days. They define students, and because no one looks deeper, there is no other way of seeing when the scores are off base.

I fought my technology test results. Many do not fight—they are not empowered to do so, and the scores swallow them whole. I've always wondered how many students fail to graduate because of the "tab" buttons in their lives. It's why grades and tests should never define students.

If I define them by their grades and tests, the tab button gets to win. Nearly every time. That's not a fail for the student. It's a fail for the system at large.

M y first week on the job, I went to the teaching store to buy decorations for my new classroom. I scanned the store. They had an endless supply of smiling apples and plan books with pictures of happy animals, sunshine, and flowers.

I was a going to be a high school teacher in a regional urban school system. I needed something less... happy. I'm a happy person, don't get me wrong, but stepping into the teacher store made me overdose on encouragement. Stickers with "Let's try harder next time!" I wanted a sticker that said, "You bombed this one" or a stamp that said, "Mediocre." I'm a firm believer in telling it like it is. Each kid has a talent. I'll find it. Sometimes their work is just plain bad. It's my job to deliver this news, and if they're really struggling, to help them out. My job is not to put a sticker on every paper.

Even the grade books in the teacher store had smiley faces. Not all grades make me want to smile.

"May I help you?" The employee looked very happy. I bet she wouldn't get mad in a classroom ever, even if a kid said the "f" word or texted during class.

"Do you have anything less... happy?" I asked.

"What do you mean?" she asked.

"Well, if I put that apple border in my room I'm going to be tossed out the window and bounced off the pavement. I need something dark and gloomy. Maybe some vampires or sad faces... And some stickers that are honest."

Her face cracked. This was the first time she had ever not smiled. I saw smoke coming out of her ears. She didn't even know the name for this emotion. Anger? Even still, she wasn't trained to yell at me. She could only say things like, "We don't say such things."

I hate "we." I say, "You need to knock that off before I fail your grandchildren." Who knows, maybe I'll be around that long.

She smiled. The "I'm calling your mother" smile.

"No. We don't have anything like that. We feel encouragement is the best way to teach."

I thanked her and left before the encouragement suffocated me. I tell kids, "Your boss won't be as encouraging as me. Do your work."

I never got my stickers that said "mediocre." But I didn't buy the smiling apples, either. I smile at my students instead. Personally. And I care. And they care in return. Together, we do great things, without smiling apples that make us want to choke.

HOW TO INCREASE TEACHER TURNOVER: THE SOVIET LABOR CAMP EQUATION

I was warned about this, and it's true—new teachers get the worst schedules. Teachers who have "paid their dues" get good schedules because schedules are often based on seniority. New teachers get what's left. New teachers should have easier classes to teach so they can learn the ropes without the additional pressures of holding the world together. Experienced teachers are equipped to handle some of the more difficult classes.

Giving new teachers the most challenges is not a recipe for training and maintaining good employees. Teachers shouldn't have to sink or swim. They need a life raft so they can develop their craft.

A lot of teachers sink. This costs the nation more than we tend to measure.

The business world recognizes the expense of hiring and maintaining the best employees. There's the cost of the search and interview process, the initial training, the mistakes new employee makes—it all boils down to dollars and cents. The time spent by other employees helping, mentoring, picking up the slack while the new person gains traction—that's money.

When it levels out and the employee's on his or her feet, there's huge payback assuming you hired the right person. That's when you want to keep your employees long-term. They are the face and backbone of the organization. They make it profitable. Employee turnover does the opposite—it spirals down to customers, and the community.

Education doesn't seem to be running these numbers in the same way businesses do. Rather than gunning for experienced employees and a stable organization, many schools look for less expensive teachers to keep the bottom line lower.

New teachers cost less. They end up doing more work. Many burn out and more new teachers come in. Since they're replaceable and there's a constant supply, nobody worries about the fact a high percentage of new teachers don't stick around to become the experienced employees who will keep the school strong. On the surface it seems to be a budgetary win—getting cheaper employees who do more work. It's not. It's more like the economic equation for a labor camp.

It's how the Soviet gulags worked. The goal was to treat prisoners just well enough to get the most work out of them before they died. Shooting them outright wasn't very effective. No work got done. The object was to maximize work and bust through five-year plan goals.

Treating prisoners too well—overfeeding them, for example—was expensive, therefore economically inefficient. People had to be fed something or they'd die too quickly or be too sick to work. If you were the commandant of the camp, you fed "guests" just enough to be productive. No more. It cut into the profits.

I saw a graph of this once, the efficiency curve for the treatment of Soviet prisoners. It marked off a point of maximum efficiency where treating prisoners just well enough to keep them alive produced maximum work output—the golden point on the graph.

This can't be the same equation in education. I've never quite understood why new teachers get paid half of what experienced teachers get then burned out by the system. We have the same workloads. We share the same kids. New teachers need to be treated like gold so they last long enough to become the experienced teachers we need.

Human resources cannot be treated like expendable commodities. Teacher burnout and turnover are currently accepted as par for

54

the course. Teachers have the highest burnout rate in the nation, above that of police and firefighters. Unless we put programs in place to stop this, our schools will never be organizations that reach for the stars.

New teachers must be treated like the heroes they are, not fed to the sharks. They are not replaceable just because they're inexpensive.

They're diamonds in the rough.

Teacher burnout rates are high because it's so easy to crash and burn in teaching. Most teachers walk through the doors to impart knowledge—they are truly passionate about their material. Somewhere along the way passion gets shuffled into a maze of testing, vocabulary words, standardization, and overload. Committees, coaching, professional development workshops... It's like the old military school adage, "Look to your left. Look to your right. At the end of the year, one of those people will be gone." Except in teaching it takes a couple of years and the rate's bit higher.

Burnout comes when a person is overloaded and doesn't know what to do. I didn't want students to feel I couldn't handle things when I was a first-year teacher. I didn't want peers to think so either, so I never asked for help. Being a first-year teacher is hard.

I was lucky. As a second-career person, I'd dealt with millions of dollars, negotiated with attorneys and body shops, written professional letters, cold called, investigated, and worked with all kinds of people. I wasn't twenty-one, right out of college, barely a year or two older than the students I was trying to teach. I had skills many new teachers didn't. It helped.

Still, I looked young. I remember I got two detentions in graduate school observing schools.

"What are you doing in the hall?" was the first one. The hall teacher apologized for the initial dose of abruptness. She was just there to make sure nobody got an unauthorized drink at the water fountain.

The second detention was from the vice principal herself at another school. I came in the side door of the office at eight on the dot as instructed.

"What are doing in the office? Why did you use that door? Why aren't you in homeroom?" I wondered if she needed another coffee and if I should offer her mine.

I let that woman yell for about five minutes. Ironically, for part of that time, she yelled about respect. I wondered how her students felt about her, whether they showed her respect—it didn't seem like she had much for them. When she finally came up for air, I smiled. A big smile. My best professional smile.

"I didn't realize graduate students could get detention." I introduced myself and extended my hand. She huffed away. Best to let people embarrass themselves, I decided, but I wondered how she affected the climate of the whole school.

Climate, I've found, contributes to teacher burnout.

First-year teachers will do anything you tell them to do—seventeen committees, coach every sport, be class advisor. After all, they don't have tenure. They can easily be let go. They get the toughest classes, do the most for the school, and rarely ask for help because they need to keep their jobs. It was my first year. My boss snuck up while I was eating lunch.

"Casey!" He never spoke. He boomed. Like a skilled dentist who waits until the instruments are solidly planted in the mouth to ask a question, he started the conversation. I was defenseless. My mouth was full of sandwich. "I have a problem."

One thing a first-year teacher with a mouth full of sandwich does not want to hear is her boss has a problem. I moved the food to one side as best I could and tried to muffle a response.

"Huh?"

He loomed over me and paused. The kind of pause that makes a person predisposed to being paranoid extremely paranoid, monkey mind running in circles. Did I do something wrong? Was I underperforming? A few of my classes were really big—were they out of control?

He postured and spoke. "The freshmen... don't... have... an advisor."

Not being fired? Relief. I choked down my bite and nodded agreement to a four-year sentence as class advisor while I was trying to hang onto the ropes and learn to teach.

Experienced teachers warned me of this. "They'll ask you to do a lot. Say no. Get settled into teaching." "No" was impossible.

Though I had a tough class load as a first-year, I was lucky to have started my career when standards were suggestions, curricula were guides—I had the freedom to teach what I wanted and, more importantly, what students requested. There were no high-stakes standards and no annual teacher evaluations full of boxes and checkmarks. If I was lucky, someone observed me once every seven years. But that someone was him.

In retrospect, it was a nice break-in period. Still, I never asked for help. Plenty of experienced teachers would've helped me. I didn't want to look weak.

A weak moment in teaching is seldom allowed. Anything less than perfection causes behind the back whispers. Being weak can sink a career.

And so "trial by fire" turns into the highest burnout rate by profession in the country. It's tough to get the best people teaching that way, tougher still to keep the best of the best.

DON'T SNIFF THE GLUE

I can sniff out a student teacher a mile away. They have piles of goodies—candy, art supplies, bells, whistles, costumes, all sitting on statements on Mastercards and Visas which will soon shoulder the weight of student loans. They have a million and one props gathered for a forty-minute lesson. Kids either love them or eat them alive. A bad student teacher makes us suffer. A good student teacher makes us all look bad.

I was at the art store. I spotted two college-aged women scrambling frantically in the adhesive aisle. There was enough glue there to repair every broken toy in America. My basket was full. Glue was only five cents. They were the August doorbusters—

corporate charity to get teachers in the door. I was hoarding. A
small country wouldn't use this much glue after an earthquake,
but any teacher knows you don't pass up supplies below a
certain price point. I don't care if it's sandpaper. I'll trade it for
something. School is one giant black market. Buy everything.
Trade later. Teachers don't get supplies. The black market is how
schools work.

"Oh my God, it's not here!" said the first woman. She was
scouring.

"What are you looking for?" I asked.

"Glue." said the second woman. How could they miss the Sears
Tower of five-cent glue two feet away?

"It's right here." I pointed.

"No, not THAT kind, THIS one." She unrolled a list of overpriced
supplies I wouldn't buy if Bill Gates wrote me a blank check.

"This glue's the same," I advised, "but nearly free." I said. "I try
not to sniff it too often." They didn't laugh, only a brief pause.
Back to the scramble. There is no humor in desperation.

"No, she said we *need* this glue."

She.

I immediately knew. "Who?" I asked anyway.

"Our student teacher supervisor." They were sentenced to finding overpriced glue because a person who hadn't been in a classroom for decades issued a royal decree.

The only help I could give was a small word of comfort.

"I'm sorry. You'll be in your own class soon. Don't let this stuff get you down. You'll do things your way. And you'll be right." I wanted them to understand that. It happened to me, too.

I was once told I'd never succeed because I didn't copy enough papers.

"You need to plan weeks in advance," she said.

I planned farther than that. Trouble was, I never knew which students would understand. I learned a lesson plan couldn't be cast in stone and, like a good performer, I had to be responsive to my audience. Copying papers weeks in advance to match lesson plans I wasn't sure would spark my audience's attention was wasteful. The trick, I found, was to tweak my drafts a couple days ahead of time in direct response to my students' reaction. It worked like a charm.

"You won't succeed." That was the feedback I received—words I have never said to another human were directed at me. Sadly, I believed them.

I believed them for too long. These types of people are wrong. Author Stephen Pressfield calls this "resistance." Recognizing resistance is the tough part. It often comes from places we don't suspect, even people close to us. When we recognize resistance for what it is—other people projecting their thoughts, issues, even caring concerns on us, the rest is easy.

The type of glue I buy doesn't matter. The number of copies doesn't matter. What matters is I love each and every student in my class, and I help them succeed. They are given to me as a gift. I give them the best I have in return.

I wanted these women to know their thoughts mattered.

Teacher prep programs shouldn't be, "My way or the highway."

No amount of shopping lists, hoops, or books about blank slates prepares a person for a kid staring him down. The only thing that works is being in the classroom, and having the heart, soul, and courage to teach. The glue—it doesn't matter so much in the end.

That's something our teacher training programs need to understand and model.

ALL THE WORLD'S A STAGE CREATING THE CHARACTER

13

Nothing prepared me for Day One of teaching. Role-playing didn't. Piles of observations and case studies didn't. The thing that prepared me for the classroom was—the classroom. I stepped onto the stage.

Teaching isn't as much about "teaching" as it is becoming a character, about using the character to convince students to learn. I left my old "Casey" at the door and assumed a character with the same name. With twenty-five eyes staring at me from the footlights to the nosebleed section and the curtain rising on opening night, the question became, "Who do I want to be?"

66

Any actor creating a character will tell you unless they are working on an impersonation so intense they lose themselves completely, the character layers itself on top of what is already there. Pieces of the actor's natural persona shine through.

Teaching is no different. It's writing a screenplay. I check my identity at the door. I become "Mrs.-Miss-Ms. So and So." Students leave class talking about my character. "I *love* that class! Her class is AWESOME." "I can't believe she did that!" I lose myself in the character. It becomes me. My character's given monologues and done improv, stand-up, and stunts. It's dived over desks, fallen on its face, caught live birds with potato chip bowls, and exploded cans of Orange Crush from ten feet away.

"How do you do that?" they ask.

"Chi." I reply. I never give up secrets. A true magician seldom does.

It's hard to develop a Tony Award winning character.

Mine is named "Miss."

People think this is odd.

"Why don't they call you "Mrs. Casey-Rowe?" For a student, "Miss" is the ultimate sign of respect—"ma'am" as it were. When they really trust me, they call me by the single last name

67

"Casey." It's how I know I've built the relationship.

A person hasn't made it in life until they only have one name. Cher. Prince. Madonna. And me. Miss. Or Casey. A rock-star moment.

"All the world's a stage," said Shakespeare. The classroom's the biggest of all. A new screenplay every day, one-hundred-eighty days a year. Lots of screenwriting. I thought my job *would be to teach*—to transfer knowledge from my brain to theirs.

No.

My job is not to teach. It is to entertain.

"*Edutain.*" I first heard this term years ago from a woman named Melody Schulman who used it in her "Little Ninjas" martial arts program for preschoolers. Schuman began as a Mouseketeer. She knew the value of entertaining. Teaching preschoolers is active— physical comedy—a little like being a Keystone Cop.

High school students want to be edutained, too. They don't learn when they're asleep, and they're powerful—they can sleep with their eyes open. I have to be interesting.

Adults are no different, yet we expect students to be. The best classes or workshops I ever took edutained me. I learned without realizing I was learning.

When I edutain, kids remember for years.

"Remember you chased the chicken?" I kicked a stuffed bird around the room like a Vaudeville routine for a lesson on hunter-gatherer societies.

"Remember you got the plague?" I'd drawn pox all over myself with Expo markers. That day, I learned Expo markers erase from boards, not bodies. I had "the plague" for a week.

"Remember when you dressed like a ninja?" It was a samurai, not a ninja, but everyone remembered college-level lessons on feudal Japan.

"Remember when you…"

They remember. Forever.

The best teachers step across the threshold with a smile as big as a Hollywood actor on the red carpet. They shake hands, make connections, become larger than life. Kids want to learn.

When I overhear students talking about my class and they say, "I love this class," that's my Tony Award. When they complain, it's my bad review in the New York Times.

Each and every day, I stand in front of the footlights, and I perform again.

WORDS MATTER

If my character matters when I step into the classroom, my words matter more. As a teacher, my words affect the life of another human being. A simple conversation—intentional or otherwise—can change pathways, for better or for worse.

In college, I wanted to get my Ph.D. I'd thought I'd research and teach. I loved history, literature, digging into archives. I really didn't know what else there was to do.

College was financially difficult for me—I found myself double-majoring in waitressing, working full-time at a minimum, doing my coursework on the side.

"You're not cut out for graduate school," said one of my two advisors. "You'll never make it. University of Michigan? Their history program's great. It's not for you..."

I believed him. I took an insurance job instead.

It was a good job. It molded me, taught me, and developed me, but I traveled that road because I did not believe I could be a great academic. My advisor chose my path with his words. A couple of sentences can change the course of a life.

As a teacher, I have that power every day.

Confidence is the smallest ember, much easier to extinguish than to kindle. Every word I say either fans the fire or blows it out. That's a big responsibility. The weight of the world, actually.

My other advisor taught through empathy.

I missed class one day. Skipped, actually. Everyone except premed students skips a class or two in college. Premed students can't skip because if they do, they miss information and people die.

"Sorry, I was out on vein and artery day... chuck this guy in with the cadavers..."

No one would die because I didn't discuss *Anna Karenina* in class or wrote a report based on the movie. I was tired. I stayed home. The phone rang. It was my advisor.

"You weren't in class today. I hope you're feeling better." I'd been caught. I was deeply embarrassed yet touched by the call. I never skipped again. Only later did I discover this professor knew my situation. He tried to help in any way he could. Instead of telling me I was a failure *because* I was working full-time, he gave me the room to succeed. I wanted to do well because he noticed and cared. I worked harder. I wanted him to be proud.

Having that one person out there who notices… who cares… It's important in the classroom, and in life as well. I observe people who make a difference in the lives of others—people who, with a single word, change lives and through that change the world. It amazes me. That's who I want to be.

The thing is, this power can go in either direction.

Any single word can be the one that changes a life forever—it can send a person toward the stars or the skids. It's the true power of teaching.

I didn't apply for the University of Michigan. Life turned out pretty well, but I wonder what my course would've been had I'd gone to graduate school immediately. Or, better yet, if that professor said, "You've been working a lot. Are you okay? You'd need to get funding and really focus on grad school if you want to go to Michigan." Or, "How will this PhD serve you? What would you *do* with it?" He would have been able to dig deeper and discover I probably didn't need a PhD but didn't know any differently. It's the train we're all on when we're at top schools. Must... get... PhD.

If he'd asked those questions, he could've said, "Here's some ideas you may not have considered. I think you'll love them. You don't really need a PhD. You're tired of debt. Let me help you use your talents in a different way."

I have this conversation with my students. "If you could wake up every day and love going to work, what types of things would you do?" I give them examples from my life now. Things I love. Things that make me get out of bed and celebrate a Monday rather than curse it.

I find they, like college me, don't have a clue about the possibilities—they only see one or two roads out of the thousand. My job is to hand out road maps and direct traffic. Get kids on a path that makes sense, so they can get up every day and celebrate Mondays, too.

If my professor had that talk with me, I'd have skipped the PhD with a smile and gone to conquer the world. That's not what happened, though. He chuckled and told me I couldn't hack it. I was embarrassed. Deflated. I looked up to him. I wanted to be a real researcher and writer, too. I wanted him to respect my work.

73

I wasn't smart enough. I couldn't hack it. I couldn't achieve at that level. I couldn't do it… It must be true. One of the academics I most respected told me so.

It takes a moment—a single word, a fragment of a sentence—to build someone up. Or destroy them completely. A posture. An offhanded remark. An attitude. As a teacher, mentor, guide… *What I say matters.* Not only in the classroom, but on the street as well.

It took me years and a few coincidences to understand he was wrong. Everyone has his or her own agenda. Ego. People put others down to feel more powerful themselves. Sometimes they have the best intentions, trying to save someone they love from a difficult path. Other times, they want to look better themselves. The end result's the same. Words change people's lives.

Now, I understand. I forgive. But it took decades to mature and shake off the power of those words. It took powerful words from others and the willingness to do the hard work to reshape my world. And for that reason I respect this power.

If I haven't used it to build someone up every single day, I've done something wrong.

15

YOU WILL NEVER BE A DOCTOR

Sometimes teachers guide students with the best of intentions but students don't understand.

I wanted to dissect a fetal pig. My biology teacher said sure, so I took the scalpel and sliced into the skin. Formaldehyde filled the air, guts sprung out like snakes from peanut brittle cans. I flipped through the book that was supposed to identify the guts. No luck. Must not be major organs. Better to ignore them. I flicked them aside. I found the heart. There's no mistaking the heart, even one gone cold. I pinned it to the cardboard. Beginner's luck. I tossed aside more things I couldn't identify. It all looked like fetal pig hamburger. I was thinking about med school.

This might look bad on the application.

"Casey, what are you doing?" He towered above my knife.

"Dissecting."

"Dissecting what?"

"This fetal pig, Colonel." I called him Colonel. In reality he'd been a captain, but also, I thought, a veteran of eight or nine wars, starting with the War of 1812. He looked like a colonel to me—someone who took no nonsense or prisoners. He wasn't my biology teacher, but he liked me. He appreciated good kids learning more about biology on their own time. He did not appreciate this dissection.

What I was seeing was the results of two distinct eras of teacher preparation. My biology teacher was a product of the "explore and do" sixties. The Colonel's formative days were the American Revolution. My teacher allowed us to explore. The Colonel required battle plans.

"What's your plan?" he asked.

I told him again. "Dissection." Perhaps it wasn't a plan so much as an action. My scalpel hacked away. I'd finished the eel and the frog the week before. Next, I thought, I'd do the cat. There were lots of dead things in jars and freezers to explore.

77

"Well, Colonel, my plan is to finish dissecting this pig."

I hacked more guts, putting them in the pile of "things I won't identify later."

"NO! YOUR PLAN!"

What more did this man want? I could only repeat myself.

He could only jump up and down. "Your paper, your outline, your write up!" Battle plans. A rolled up sheet brought to the general by a courier who waited for approval. With pictures with circles and arrows and a paragraph on the back of each one explaining what each one was…

I sighed. Who needs to draw pictures? They're in the book.

"Oh, I don't have that. It's all in my head." I was staying after school doing extra biology on my time because I wanted to learn. What idiot teacher would get kids to do that if he said, "Hey, thanks for coming. Here's a twenty-page a lab report template…"

We did lab reports as part of class. They weren't fun. I got them back with smileys. Once in a while one would be returned with the worst possible indictment, "I'm disappointed in your efforts," or "You didn't work to your potential."

It was a knife through my soul. I'd let him down. Nothing was worse than this. I worked harder. Now I'm the one writing smileys and indictments on papers wishing we didn't have grades at all, just kids who stayed after because they want to learn.

I didn't realize it at the time, but my biology teacher developed "intrinsic learning." I wanted to learn for the sake of learning. But the Colonel was right, too. Sometimes a little organization goes a long way when making a lesson stick. As a teacher, I try to create an environment that blends both these things, organizing the material, but leaving room for kids to suggest, dig deeper, and explore.

I continued my dissection. The Colonel shook his head with disgust.

"This is awful. I hope you don't plan to be a doctor. You'll kill people."

I looked up. I *did* plan to be a doctor, that week, anyway. It's one of the two or three careers smart-ish kids know we should be. We're not sure what else to aspire to at sixteen. We're supposed to go to college and be doctors, lawyers, or stockbrokers. I had the grades to pull off medicine, not the work ethic. People would've died.

So the next week I decided I'd go to college for International Relations. World peace was kind of like medicine but it kept even more people alive, if I didn't mess that up, too, starting a regional or global conflict in the process. After a few months, I decided on something else after realizing that diplomacy was nothing more than professional ass-kissing. And so it goes when you're eighteen.

When you get sick, you can thank the Colonel I'm not your doctor.

Years later, I discovered he was a master gardener. He gave me advice for growing vegetables. I think of him in the spring when I'm avoiding bugs and overcrowding my peas. He wouldn't like my overcrowded peas. Not in the battle plans.

Sometimes when teachers guide students, they do it with fifty years of experience and love. They've fought the fights, and they have a good idea about human nature. They gently guide kids to where they're supposed to be, recognizing each has a unique talent and gift, knowing there's a place in the world for them.

As adults, we, those kids, realize life would have been easier if we'd listened the first time. Now I'm busy trying to convey these messages to the next generation—my years of experience, my battle scars. I want my students to avoid the struggle. I hope they listen much better than high school me. But they don't. They struggle. And they make their way until one day they return and say, "I wish I listened to you earlier."

They couldn't. Nor could high school me. Revelations come in their own due time.

Struggling, I found, is the only way the real lessons—the "essence of life" lessons—stick.

APOLOGY

I had a teacher in high school who couldn't spell "Einstein" or "magic." I didn't want to take his class. I needed it. It was one of those "You-Need-This-For-College" classes that no kid ever knows why.

He made mistakes on the board and typos on paper. Students corrected him. He'd apologize. Mistakes didn't seem to bother him. They bothered me. He was the expert. How could experts make mistakes?

He tried to organize me.

"You need to take good notes to succeed. You don't take good notes," he said. True, but I liked my notes—my scribbles on pages transported me back to the lecture, little time machines. He'd say, "You have to follow the system!" His system was beautiful. Tables of contents with neatly attached pages... mine couldn't be read, except by me.

When I studied... if I studied... I used my notes. I stared at the doodles. It was a "system" that carried me through high school, college, grad school—a single marble composition book for each semester with scribbles bringing me back in time. It's how I operate even today. It wasn't "the required system." The "required system" left me stranded. I'd leave notebooks all over the place. I always had the wrong one in my hand.

I ran into this teacher later in life. I discovered that as an adult, I liked him very much. He saw a disaster like me–backpack barfing, squashed banana in my locker, bad fashion, generally on a planet other than my own. He tried to avert disaster with the best tools in his box.

Focus. Organization. Systems. These, he had in abundance.

What he needed was flexibility—flexibility to recognize which things were effective for me—that my way of learning, though different, was valid. His thoughts were linear. Mine were a spiderweb, each casting a line to several others, weaving together. There was a rhyme and reason to my thoughts. The way I organized my systems held them all together.

It's an important lesson—one I put in my bag of tricks. Sometimes, I find, students are on point, even when they appear to be a mess. And so, rather than imposing my systems, I take the time to ask about theirs.

"I see your backpack is barfing with papers. How can I help?" Sometimes it's just their way. Other times, they're completely lost. I show them a notebook from my past. It puts them at ease. If I have succeeded, despite this notebook, they can succeed. Together, we arrive at a system that works.

One day, I was teaching. I was having a mistake-filled day.

"Miss, you forgot to close the quotations on the sentence." Indeed I had.

"Miss, you did that math wrong." I couldn't find my mistake.

Math Friend Next Door said, "Yup, you missed a step." If my job is to make students better than me, I was having a good afternoon. I high-fived math kid and gave him candy.

I noticed something, though. He looked at me the same way I looked at the teacher who misspelled Einstein and magic. Like I was stupid. Like he was questioning my value as a professional and a human being.

I invented that look. I also earned the karma. I'd have a long way to go to get that kid back. It took time. I wonder how history will write my reviews.

Teachers aren't supposed to be real people. We're supposed to be perfect. I keep forgetting that and messing up. Suddenly, every teacher who made an impact on me, good or bad, flashed before my eyes and I realized they were human. And I'm human, too.

Maybe if I have one more cup of coffee, I'll be a better human better today.

BREAKING SOME RULES

I got tickets to an innovation conference. I was excited. Teachers don't get tickets to places where people exchange business cards. Most teachers don't even have business cards. Business cards, I think, are a measure of importance. I had them in my prior lives. They had little logos next to my name, official position, and contact information. I'd give them out to cool and important people who'd give me one and we'd never really look at them again, but for a brief moment, we exchanged something. Status.

Society hasn't deemed teachers worthy. On the rare occasion someone wants our information, we scrawl it on Post-It notes, but no one ever calls us unless a kid's failing. We don't go to swanky affairs like I did in business, and we certainly don't get invited to really expensive conferences—the kind where people eat, drink, and shake hands, exchanging cards. One day, I was talking to a woman at a local event. I wrote my email on a Post-It note and ripped it off the top. My partner in crime snuck up behind me.

"Stop that!" he said.

"Stop what?" I inquired.

"Writing your info on sticky notes. It's not classy. Get some damned business cards!"

"Teachers don't have business cards."

"You're out in public now. Make some." The thought never occurred to me that I had the power to make my own business cards. I was hanging with a crowd of innovators now. Old-school thinking was out. My friend had the coolest card ever, "I Work Because I Love This Shit."

I wondered if I could get away with a card like that. I didn't think I should put "shit" on my card, though, I am a teacher after all, so I picked my favorite ten quotes and slapped my name, number, blog, and Twitter handle on the back. It was more symbolic than anything—the moment the cards came in the mail, I felt like a real person. I was ready to return to the world, the world where people network over beer and have ideas they execute, rather than letting them die in committee or, worse yet, getting executed for having ideas.

And now I was at a super swanky conference—a conference for big ideas.

I looked at the impressive speaker lineup. The person I really wanted to see was Carmen Medina—former Deputy Director of Intelligence for the Central Intelligence Agency.

I was going to see a real, hard-core spy.

She didn't look threatening when she arrived on stage. I expected her to Jason Bourne her way out and maybe shoot someone with a laser gun. She didn't. Instead of spy stories, she talked about rebels—how rebels are the people who fix organizations that can't seem to get out of their own way. Organizations shouldn't ignore them. They should embrace them.

Rebels? Aren't those the people we eliminate?

"Rebels," she said "are not the enemy." That, I didn't expect to hear.

"Rebels love their organizations and want them to be their best. They're the people who take them to the next level." She was talking to me. She looked right at me. She must've been reading my email. No, wait, that was the other organization.

"Most rebels are not trained to do it properly." It's why we burn out.

She was right. Fighting windmills gets me nowhere.

Really great people get derailed and beaten down by bureaucracy and organizational ineffectiveness. Then they stop trying to innovate change, or worse yet, leave. Creating change is an art.

"Bad rebels break rules. Good rebels change them." I was tempted to say, "You've obviously never worked in public education." But then I remembered the CIA is a government agency. Could changing education be more difficult than tackling the federal government? Probably not.

We can, as Mahatma Gandhi said, "Be the change we want to see" at any level. Then, each of us—a single drop of change—trickles into a stream, flows into a river, and before long we, once isolated molecules, are all part of the ocean. Together.

A friend of mine is a successful entrepreneur. He asked, "How do you get anything done as a teacher?"

"By circumventing blockades and hiding," I said.

"I like that." "Sometimes you have to break the rules. It's good for you."

89

Carmen says no. *Don't break the rules. Change the rules.* I'm a rule follower. But sometimes, I get pushed, especially when I see how "the rules" hold my students back.

I'm not Gandhi or Martin Luther King. I'm just a teacher who finally got fed up and made her own business cards.

As a teacher, it's all about connecting with students, but it's also about courage. I teach about courageous people. Sometimes I have to be one, even if the system frowns—especially then. I'm not sure how to get education to make sense. Break rules, or change them? Which is the chicken, and which is the egg?

Maybe I'll figure it out before I get scrambled.

A GOOD EXAMPLE OF A BAD BOOK

Often the best lessons are not the ones I expect to teach or learn. I was taking a seminar called "The Presidents" in graduate school. We were drinking coffee in the professor's parlor. He held the seminar in his living room, like Socrates would've done, but with coffee, not hemlock.

"Tell me how you liked the book." The professor was an old-style academic from the Midwest, who had completed his masters' degree at the university where I'd been an undergraduate.

"Well, I thought the insight the author showed into the presidents was very intriguing," said one student. He went on to outline the revelations he received from the book in unabridged detail. I was confused. Did he accidentally read the Bible?

"It was good," said another. "I thought last week's was better, but I enjoyed it." No further details. She wouldn't commit.

We went around the circle, a few saying little or even passing on their turn, one or two giving adulations. Others were shifting in their seats, squirming. They wanted to say something, but couldn't bring themselves to do it.

"And what about you, Dawn?" I hesitated. I'd had a very different experience with this book.

"Um," I looked around the room. Half a dozen pens and notebooks were at the ready, as they tended to be in graduate school prior to laptops and iPads. "I thought this was the worst book I've ever read."

Silence. One gasp, from the guy who read the Bible.

"Go on," the professor said, his face void of emotion. It was too late to put the top back on the can of worms. I continued.

"Well," I said, "The author doesn't seem to have any academic credentials in this field—I researched him—but that's not my issue. I might've still enjoyed it. Lots of experts can't afford degrees." I named a colonial scholar who wrote on the subject of witch trials. He left Yale without a PhD, but was still an authority on the subject. "You don't need a PhD for me to read you."

I looked around the room. The kid who read the Bible was ready to attack.

I bent down pulling the offending manuscript from my bag.

"Look," I said leafing through the circled text and notes in the margin. "Spelling errors. Editing errors, and I'm not sure this event," I opened to a page, "ever happened," noting one historical event I'd questioned.

"Also, what's his thesis? I couldn't find it… he was so vague. I couldn't nail it down. My mind drifted. Sorry. I just didn't like this book." I listed a couple of others I did like, historians that gave me deep insights into dead presidents.

Silence. Pause. One or two potential scholars sat waiting for the lambasting I'd set in motion.

"Congratulations. You got the answer!" he exclaimed. "THIS… is a good example of a really bad book." The professor excoriated the book, telling us how horrible it truly was. "Sometimes you need to look at the worst of the worst to appreciate the best."

We'd just learned a solid lesson as historians.

I do this exercise with my students. I give them something of dubious quality then ask their thoughts. Sometimes, a kid stands up for his or her belief in the face of those who'll say what they think I want to hear. Those are our future leaders. Experts. Entrepreneurs. Maybe even a live president or two.

Education isn't about manufacturing a bunch of minions. It's about developing keen minds with confidence—people who refuse to be yes men. These are the students who will innovate and iterate the solutions for the future. They will stand and speak the truth even when the truth is not popular.

They will change the world.

"A good example of a bad book" works everywhere—it's true for life as well. When something goes wrong, when life doesn't turn out well—that's the bad book. Accept the lessons as gifts. The bad books teach us as much as the good books if we read them right.

That was one of the most valuable lessons I learned in school.

Ever.

WHY CAN'T WE ALL GET ALONG?

Teaching would be easier if the adults all got along.

"You know," he said, "It's people like you who make it difficult for us. You and your technology. I have to enforce the rules with my students and they break them with you. The union is never going to back you, and I wouldn't be surprised if you end up with your tires slashed one day."

My crime—I'd dared, in passing, to compliment a colleague's QR code. I had a QR code once, a little square students could scan to get homework or receive inspirational messages on the way into the room. Students liked it. But "no phones," applied to homework messages and inspirational quotes, too.

"What's that square? They can't use phones." I'd been discovered.

"Well, it's for homework, this way they can use an app to add it to their calendars, set an alarm, and not forget."

"Phones aren't allowed. They can use their agendas." Agendas are little paper books where kids can record homework. Mostly they use them for lav passes, yet we spend a ton of money on them. One or two out of my two hundred students use them for their intended purpose. We can save big bucks by buying leather-bound planners held by personal assistants for the two students who learn best that way, and spend the money we save on things we really need.

"They don't use their agendas. They hate them. I haven't used a paper planning system for fifteen years."

I showed the empty agendas littering the floor and shelves—wasted money and resources. It costs nothing to let students use their smartphones for schoolwork.

"What about the digital divide?" one administrator asked years ago when I made the argument for permission to let students use their own technology. "Some kids are poor. That's not fair."

What's not fair, I thought, is preparing kids for a world that existed fifty years ago.

I took exception to the "poor" thing, recalling the years my mom had to hunt for half-used pencils on the first day of school. I wasn't rich. Not only that, personal technology wasn't invented, so we all fell into the category of unfortunate students who had to Shanghai a parent to drive forty-five minutes to a college library. There, we sat at tables reading actual books and taking notes on index cards. Yet we finished our papers.

"I used consider that," I said. "Here's the thing. I'm the least suc-cessful of all my friends." She gasped. No one says such things in education. We all say things like "You're great," and "I know you can do it." No one really calls it like it is.

"I'm not saying I suck." We also don't say things like "suck." "I'm just saying my friends are successful. And they say things like, 'Public education stinks. Send me an employee I can work with, not someone who's entitled and goes home at the dot of five o'clock asking for a raise without finishing the work.'"

I smiled at her. "I overcame challenges growing up. I got my stuff done. My students need to, too. They'll find access to a computer, even if I give them extra time. If they have challenges, they'll be all the better for it—they're the employees I'd hire. They're the ones I'd pass on to my friends."

I didn't win. Students still couldn't use their phones for school.
One old-timer even went so far as to suggest all faculty and staff
should be stripped of their phones. I said I'd quit on the spot—
not because I love my phone, but because I have 2.5 degrees
telling me I've earned certain privileges in life. Being treated
like an adult and professional is one.

That was years ago. And now, I found a colleague my resur-
rected the QR code, bringing secret messages to life once more. I
had complimented her. I would've skipped the compliment if I'd
known I had to wear protective armor. I turned to leave.

Then I heard the other person say, "Our kids aren't mature
enough. They can't handle it," and something about drug dealers
using phones.

"How are my fifteen-year olds are less 'able to handle it' than
fifteen-year olds in charter or private schools whose communities would never stand for no technology?"

He'd hit a nerve. "Separate but equal" doesn't work in the
American educational system when we create conditions where
one group gets more privileges than another.

I assured my colleague that while I obeyed school rules I was
out to change them. Not just for me, but for all schools. We can't
have pockets of privilege and permission in some areas where
others are on lockdown. We need to give all students the tools

they require to succeed, not create conditions of inequity where some students have the world at their fingertips and others only broken equipment, blocked sites, and banned technology.

The ironic thing is many schools are finally getting technology only because the new wave of standardized tests requires it. In any case, I'll take it.

If we don't educate kids with the most progressive methods and technology we can, we're saying—literally or de facto, "I know you need this for life. I choose not to prepare you."

Many people fear technology—they think kids will do something bad. They probably will. We did bad things in school. Kids can be good or bad without technology. Schools need to create a climate where people are kind and supportive of each other—from the adults on down.

Then, we can teach.

Because of the controversy around tech, it's become a real social justice issue. When some schools ban it and other schools bless it, it creates conditions where students receive different qualities of education.

"Broken, blocked and banned," cannot be themes in education. Students cannot compete on the world stage if they haven't learned to navigate technology professionally. They'll lose opportunities to the kids who have this skill every time. Without permission to be progressive, I'll be preparing them for lower-level jobs of the past rather than cutting-edge opportunities of the future.

So, yes, it's a social justice issue—civil rights, even. Students who come from "broken, blocked, and banned" environments do not receive the same education as students who have technology. And we've already decided that "separate but equal" leaves some of the best people behind.

THE $186 BOX OF PAPER

I f every kid can't have a laptop, phone, and tablet in class, I'm going to need more paper. Teachers know this feeling—constantly having to beg for basic supplies. It's time consuming and embarrassing. These days, I'm pretty well taken care of. In the past, it wasn't always the case.

"I need paper, please." I said please. I don't ask for a lot.

"I'm not in charge of paper." This was a new development in requisitioning. "It seems I've been giving it out too liberally." The person formerly in charge of such things peeked into my box. "That box is empty. It's my professional opinion you need paper."

"Thank you. How do I get some?"

"Put a requisition in…"

I'd like to, but I'm teaching—two hundred fifty-four students. It's why I need paper. It's why I forget to fill out forms in triplicate, or if I do, I leave them in a pile on my desk, never putting them in the right hands. Who could be in charge now? The person in the front office? God?

I'm frugal by nature. I don't waste. When I'm running low on paper, I tell students to write smaller. I love trees and don't want to kill rainforests so American kids can be smarter.

"You there! You can write HALF that size! Tomorrow, we're using six-font on quarter-sheets of paper. DON'T give me that look! You CAN fit an essay on a stamp! Front and back! Write SMALL dammit! You call that *small?* It's not small till you fit it on a grain of rice. Do it again! WHAT? Are you INSANE? Don't take more paper. ERASE! *ERASE!"*

Requisitioning supplies makes me insane. It's gotten better over the years, but the fact there's no supply cabinet and I can't go to a copy machine without bringing my own paper—that's something I'll never get used to. In all other places of employment, I got up, got a pencil, sat down, and worked. I pushed the button on the copier. If it ran low, I refilled it as a courtesy to the next user.

Now, I make my copies and take my paper with me, making sure I don't leave a single sheet behind. This ultimately breaks the copier, too, all that opening, slamming, and ripping out paper. This requires me to take more time out of my day to fix it.

There's no supply cabinet in education. I fill out seventeen forms, hunt down a dozen signatures, and follow two days' worth of instructions. Then, I give up and go to the store. Most do. It's what the system intends. Students do without or teachers spend their paychecks on their jobs. Neither's a good solution.

The best school quartermaster knows this. Having gotten his certification in a formerly communist nation, he makes sure no one dares ask for supplies. "Are you sure you need a pencil?" Pause. I stay. "Go wait in that line." I wait. The bureaucrat shuts Window One and opens Window Two. He's behind that window, too. I protest. I'm dangerously close to not getting my pencil.

The quartermaster's role is important. He's in charge of protecting the taxpayer from people like me. I have to be nice. The fate of my world is in his hands.

I lived in Russia for a short spell. Bureaucracy was the official Russian pastime—an art, something to be appreciated. I studied every bureaucrat I encountered, envying their talent for obfuscation. For them, it was a matter of national pride, even in post-Soviet Russia. Every purchase I made in an official store—even a simple loaf of bread—required waiting in at least two lines, three if they were doing their job.

Just when I'd get to the front of the line, the place where they're supposed to say "*cledushy*," "Next," the clock would strike "lunch." Lunch is a full Soviet hour. A Soviet hour isn't sixty minutes. It's more like a basketball "five minutes" where the time outs and commercials can take days. Customers waited outside the store until lunch was over, later returning to wait in the same line again. Politely, or they wouldn't leave with bread.

I tried various ways to get supplies in the beginning of my career. My first year teaching I mumbled under my breath, "It would be NICE if I could get some board markers…"

The next day, board markers appeared. Magic. I muttered for paper. It appeared. Did I have superpowers, or was there an advanced telepathic requisitioning system? I kept muttering and ordering. Best… school… ever!

One day, I saw a student take a board marker out of his bag. He put it on my ledge. I had some tough "entrepreneurial" kids with various side operations. I tried to keep them on the right path. I told them crime didn't pay.

"Sure it does, Miss, how much did *you* make last week?"

Touché.

They looked out for me because I cared about them. I hustled basketball in return for attendance and assignments, I went to their baby showers, I listened when the toughest of the tough said, "I'm scared to live in my neighborhood." I dropkicked them to graduation. I proved they mattered. And in return, I mattered to them. They wanted me to be happy.

So things appeared. A ream of paper. A board marker. It was their way of taking care of me in the best way they knew how. I was touched. Deeply. I had their respect.

I wasn't magic, though. I was disappointed to learn I couldn't make supplies appear—that someone, somewhere, was out of a ream of paper and a board marker because I was in need.

I stopped grumbling for supplies. This method of procurement didn't seem very honest. I secretly wondered whether I could've muttered my way to a class set of computers or a new car—something really cool. I never tried. It wouldn't have been right.

It's a decade later. I go through legitimate channels for things I need. I start early and hoard. The true post-Soviet quartermaster knows this and corrects for it, adding red tape to the process. It's a cat and mouse game. A master teacher starts "procuring" the year before, and the quartermaster starts saying no. I currently have a lifetime supply of staples and paper clips if anyone wants to make a trade. If I like you, I'll give you some. That's how we make relationships in education. You know you have a true friend if they tell you the location of their secret stash.

"Didn't you get paper in September?" I was asked.

"Yes, but I also got a ton of students in September. They wrote on that paper."

I'm trying to digitize. I'm not done yet. I need students to be able to use their phones, tablets, and laptops. Meanwhile, I... must... have... paper!

I resolved to discover the *actual* cost of paper. It's nearly free at the August "Back to School" sales when every teacher shops for the year, but schools don't purchase like that, and teachers can't submit expense reports for reimbursement when they find things on sale. Most schools have approved vendors. I'm told it safeguards against favoritism and overspending. I'm not sure how spending twice as much saves money in the end. Maybe there's a coupon.

Meanwhile, I calculated the cost of the time it takes to complete the requisitioning process. I counted the time spent filling out forms, emails, checking on the process and identifying the right person. I added up the prorated value of salaries of the employees whose job it is to stop me from getting paper, and all of the wasted time. The box came in at just under two hundred dollars.

Considering the price the government is willing to pay for a coffee pot or pen that goes into space, that's really pretty cheap, making this purchase a no-brainer.

I got my box of paper. I hid it—I've had boxes stolen. Finally, I set the default font on my printer to four so I can get the *most* out of every sheet this time and contemplate a time when kids'll use technology instead of paper. Then, I looked at my watch. Time to get busy teaching once again.

Paper's not the only thing I run out of during the year. I run out of other things, too. I think school should supply the basics, but students have some responsibility to come prepared, too. Sometimes kids expect the school—and me—to give them a bit too much.

I'm out of tissues and hand sanitizer. Students are displeased. I watch them hit the lever on the sanitizer several times like a person pushing the elevator button repeatedly. It doesn't speed up.

"It was out when you got up five seconds ago," I say. They're not using it to prevent flu or because they just picked their nose. It

seems to have become sneaker cleaner and substitute for showers after gym.

"Miss, got any tissues?" I keep forgetting to bring more. There's
a stockpile in my basement. I bought a million boxes on sale
with coupons.

"No, sorry." Huff. Stomp. Sulk.

I'm indignant this student is annoyed at me. He should be prepared. Then I recognize I'm not annoyed at him. I'm annoyed at
the system. Nationwide.

I wonder why it's perceived as a teacher's job to provide everything for… our jobs.

I take a moment to regroup. Getting annoyed isn't productive.
I have a friend whose entire measure of life is "productive"
or "not productive." It's a life-changing exercise when done
religiously—brings a hundred doves worth of inner peace. Getting annoyed doesn't bring tissues. The former students who
magically procured supplies have long since graduated. Being
annoyed just makes me—well, annoyed. "Not productive." In
teaching, there are tons of things to be annoyed about every
day, set up like dominoes, ready to fall. Each, quite valid but
"not productive."

Instead, I flip the equation. I think, "I'm grateful I can afford tissues and supplies for my classroom." There was a time when I couldn't. There was a time when I ran my household on thirty dollars a week for groceries with kids still asking me for personal and class supplies.

"Miss, you got a pencil?"

"Miss, got lotion?"

"Miss, you're OUT of hand sanitizer."

"I didn't eat lunch. You got any snacks?" Students handed me grocery lists.

Eventually, I had to say no.

For two years in the middle of the biggest recession I'll ever see, I lived in fear like the rest of America. Would I lose my house? My business? After I took out twenty-five thousand dollars in graduate school loans to cut my salary in half to teach, some kids were mad I didn't buy them food and pencils.

I learned a lesson. Saying "no," to kids didn't make them love me less. Most understood. My class wasn't less valuable. We got more creative—which is what education is supposed to be all about, now, isn't it?

Thankfully, those days are over for now. I bring students treats when I can. These days aren't gone for every teacher, and I never know if they'll come back for me. I see the newest teachers stockpile because they want their classrooms to be the cornucopias students deserve. I see teachers put themselves in debt. I've been there—I have the old credit card statements to prove it. Going into debt to perform the functions of a job is never a good thing. It usually means it's time to look for a new job.

"Miss, got a Band-Aid?"

"Miss, I don't have a pencil."

"I need a notebook."

"Where's the paper?"

"Do you have markers?"

I give a thousand pens and pencils per year. Once, I saw a teacher who was marked down on her evaluation because a student didn't have a pencil. Her students "weren't prepared." The notes said she hadn't taught them to be. That's serious.

I really hope as we progress with education reform, someone budgets for a box of tissues. Because not only do I have to blow my nose once in a while, I often have to cry.

I DON'T KNOW IF I CAN DO THIS ANYMORE

❝I don't know if I can do this anymore," my friend told me. "I can't teach first graders to sit for a hundred-eighty days. I don't even have time to play with my own boys." As a teacher, whether we have twenty-five or two hundred students, they become ours. Teaching is a life calling. I've spent more time with other people's kids than my own little boy.

My friend was considering leaving. It's what happens when good a teacher looks around the room and wonders if she matters—if the red tape will continue to prevent her from creating the magic she needs to change the world. These thoughts start as seeds but grow into weeds. Teachers burnout more than police officers and doctors.

While teachers technically get summers off, there are always more requirements and regulations for certification—a week of training, curriculum writing, professional development… summers fill up fast. Before I know it, it's time to prepare for fall.

I'm left with a choice… be good to my family or do all the extras teachers are expected to do on our time.

I hate to say it, but I was a better teacher—by industry standards—before I had a family. I stayed at school until six-thirty, went to every event, and nearly adopted every kid in need. I bought them food, designed lessons, and corrected papers until two in the morning. Working from 7 a.m. to midnight made me a rock star.

Conversely, people looked down on the mom who called in sick for parent conferences. Her husband was a grad student teaching night classes, and she had no sitter for those times. Besides, that was the time she should have been reading her own kids stories after working all day not seeing them.

Society expects teachers to choose between these two roles—school or family.

I wonder if everyone feels that way?

"I just corrected two hundred essays and didn't cook my family dinner." That is an actual quote.

"I have to call in sick tomorrow to catch up on my goal paperwork and my correcting." Another quote.

Balance is important. Teachers don't have it. I've failed at "balance" my whole life. Maybe it's why I became a good teacher. Sometimes, the right answer, even in teaching, is "no."

"Sorry. That won't work." Direct. Simple. Polite.

The ability to say no and to have balance—both are game changers. These are lessons I'm still trying to get right. "No" is the answer nobody wants to hear.

It was my first career. The phone rang at my desk.

"Hello, how can I help you?" The person on the other end of the line didn't speak English. Click. Someone transferred the call. It should have been theirs. It happened to me all the time because I love languages. Still, wasn't particularly fluent in any. It took me a lot of time to help everyone else's customers, time when no one was helping mine.

"Hola. Necessito hablar con alguien…" These were real people in crisis who had car accidents. They needed help. I couldn't turn them away, even if I was getting behind.

In the days before Google Translate, every time a person got mad and shouted a word at me, I'd have to look it up in a real dictionary. "Seguro! Seguro!" *Seguro* means "insurance." A good word to know. Before long, I stopped confusing my *yantes* (tires) with my *llaves* (keys) and I improved. Still, it took a lot of time out of my day.

The better I got, the more calls came my way.

While I was taking people's calls in Spanish, Russian, Polish, Ukrainian, Hindi, and Vietnamese, the pile on my desk was growing. Finally, I'd had enough. I asked for a raise. I was saving the company tons of money. I'd split the difference and be given time in my job for this function. I'd calculated the amount I was saving, and presented it to my boss.

The response was laughter. Serious laughter. Comedy Central laughter. "Nice one, Casey. No."

"Fair enough. But I'm not translating anymore. I need to focus on my work." After that, I didn't feel like a "team player" even though translating was never part of my job to begin with. It's tough to say no in schools, too.

Sometimes saying "no" is the right thing to do. No one gets medals for it, though. Just sanity. I never quite brought that lesson to my classroom.

Life is a marathon, not a sprint. It's important to set realistic expectations, even in teaching. Especially in teaching. I want to see my son grow up. This means I can't coach, be on every committee, and join every initiative, even if I add value. I have to say no. It's hard. It's even harder to take the guilt out of the equation, because I always want to do more for students.

This year, I followed my own advice and I put the guilt back in Pandora's box where it belongs. I'm no superhuman. Starting now, I'm deciding to be a regular human.

To be honest, it feels pretty good.

In order to get, and keep, the best teachers, we need to set realistic expectations, especially in an environment where we have twenty-four hour contact capabilities and more and more that needs to get done. We need to set limits, because the best of the best shouldn't say, "I don't think I can do this anymore." They should be looking at the smiling faces and setting the pace for the future.

BARISTA DAY

It's true teachers have the highest burnout rate in the nation. Half the problem would be solved if the world showed education a little love. It's no accident that teacher burnout is on the rise at a time when media assaults educators, and friends of prospective teachers say, "You don't want to do that."

I see how far a little appreciation can go.

I have a second job. Most teachers do. My second job is in technology, a job I came into by accident when looking for teachers that "used computers in their classrooms and didn't have money." It was quite by accident. It changed the course of my life and certainly how I view teaching.

My Job Two team is some of the best and brightest in the world. I take vision from them daily. Even though they sit in an office on the other side of the nation, I feel a part of that team. Except on barista day. Teachers don't get "barista day." Truth be told, I get a little bit jealous. No one makes a cup of coffee with a little milk heart in it for me.

Teachers would know we had status in society once more if we had a "barista day" too.

I think I'll bring that up at the next faculty meeting. "Friday is barista day." The closest we come is the coffee setup I keep stocked in my room. I don't think we're getting a barista in my lifetime.

One particular day, I broke down and asked Job Two Friend about this. I learned at some companies there's an entire executive in charge of employee happiness—anticipating needs. It could be anything from providing kombucha to anticipating things an employee might need. This keeps the best and the brightest smiling, not hunting for other jobs. It decreases turnover and increases productivity. Tech people are at a premium. It's important to keep them happy.

We don't have that situation in education. It's the law of supply and demand. Teachers are not "at a premium." There are a lot of people who want to teach, so in many systems they're expendable commodities. "A dime a dozen," I've been told.

Instead of giving the best and brightest kombucha, the system gives them extra work until they become one of the burnout stats. Then, they leave for places with happiness managers. Sure, teachers are a dime a dozen—it's always possible to hire a new and less expensive teacher. The real best and brightest have other options. When they leave for companies with baristas and masseuses, though, the overall quality of education in the United States goes down.

I want to come into my class one day and see a happiness manager. "Hey, how are you feeling today? Teach a good class? You're a rock star." I don't think it's going to happen any time soon. I tried to take on the role myself. One day, I went around and brought a chocolate bar to every person in the building, an idea I stole from a friend's blog. I got hugs. One person cried. I felt good about myself, but sad about a system where simply getting a piece of candy made some people hug me and cry. We need happiness managers, stat.

During the first dot com boom, I had a friend in a Boston tech company. She tried to get me to work with her, saying tech was the future. I went to visit. It was such a cool place to be. Even then, there was an employee dedicated to buying and stocking food. I called him Captain Crunch because there always seemed to be sugar cereal around. This was far before clean eating and paleo were the norm, back when Reagan declared ketchup a vegetable. The company had video games, a hammock. Dinner was brought in at 6 p.m. every night.

"You don't understand," she said. "That's so people won't leave. The implication is we'll work twenty-four hours a day."

"But you have *fun!"* I said. I should have taken that job. I didn't have kids then. I could've worked twenty-four hours a day. Captain Crunch brought food and there was foosball and a hammock.

The happiness factor means everything.

HR shouldn't stand for Human Resources. It should stand for Happiness and Retention... in most places in education it stands for Horror Reducer...

My friend at Job Two reiterated the importance of having a good environment to keep the best people.

"It's really, really competitive."

He was right. Good people are essential to any operation. I

tipped my empty coffee cup in his general direction and got back to the work at hand—finding paper, swearing at blocked internet links, and trying to overdose on caffeine--without a barista.

I think about this conversation. "I need to keep good people. It's competitive."

Why doesn't anyone feel that way about good teachers? Why do I always hear things like, "You're tenth step with a masters. No one will ever hire you." Quality never comes into play. Being "the best" becomes irrelevant.

I looked around one more time. No barista. No happiness manager. No Captain Crunch. No kombucha. I decided to make myself one last cup of coffee, then get back to the job at hand, creating an environment that makes the best and the brightest— my students—smile and feel like the rock stars they are.

24

MY DAY

ONE SUICIDE ATTEMPT.   FOILED

ONE AMBULANCE.   DROVE AWAY.

ONE FIGHT.   DIFFUSED.

ONE UNHAPPY CUSTOMER.   SATISFIED.

ONE MIGRAINE.   DRUGGED.

ONE IPOD.   STOLEN.

ONE DOLLAR.   LENT.

ONE MOM.   GRATEFUL.

ONE STUDENT.   IN TEARS.

MIGRAINE.   DRUGGED AGAIN.

TWO MINDS.   CHANGED. MAYBE.

MORE COFFEE.

25

HEROES

The boy was asleep with his head on the desk. Pretty soundly, it seemed. I woke him again. Maybe I was boring? I asked.

"No, Miss, I had to work." He worked in his family's restaurant, often until one or two in the morning except for soccer season, because he was starting varsity.

The girl was failing. She was absent all the time and never came after school for work.

"I can't stay after school. I'm not allowed." She babysat while her mom worked. Some days this meant she stayed home.

One boy disappeared for weeks at a time. Another paid his family's rent as a sophomore.

I've had emancipated students, students shouldering adult finances, students who were undocumented and hiding. One senior had a mom who passed away in her country two months before graduation. The student was undocumented and couldn't see her before she died. Another student was a caretaker for her very ill mother. She put off college to help the family. One freshman responded to my beginning of the year survey, "What do you do for fun?" with, "I just play with my son."

It's easy to be judgmental—to avoid looking at problems kids face as they go through school, to say, "We all have problems, kid. Someday your boss will fire you if you don't get your work done. Make it happen." Try being a homeless student looking for a job.

For a kid in crisis, there's no "make it happen," only "survive today." Who am I to have the cojones to think my "critical questions" are the most important thing in this kid's life? I think of the times I was in crisis and failed to pay attention to the manila folders on my desk as an adult.

I've heard adults blast students. "These people can't keep their kids home to translate." Sometimes, the critics are the very same people who fail to show up for work themselves. It's okay to skip every Friday, and stay home to do Christmas shopping, but when a teenage girl goes to help her mom understand the doctor, that's truancy. I've heard people say, "It's illegal to let him work that late, somebody ought to turn his parents in." Had they ever been in a position where the choice was rent or food, they might have spoken differently. Or not at all. Some of these kids face problems that would cripple adults, yet they come to school, ready to do their best.

Those kids are my heroes.

Many families fight to survive. Somewhere in between, that kid tries to do your math, my critical questions, and read a text he wishes would shed light on his particular crisis so he could learn something helpful to dig his way out. Something to take away the pain. Sadly, he's given another worksheet.

Often, kids make the effort to work hard simply because they like me. They trust I'm giving them something of use. But in the midst of their chaos—where each day crumbles, I wonder—what can the education system do to be a lifelong friend—to teach students that no matter the problem, we can support them, lift them up, show them a way to make it better, one step at a time?

Education must be flexible, personalized, and human. We're taking so much time testing and standardizing the experience there's not always room to customize a best fit for students, especially students with heavy burdens to carry, and education is changing—a revolution in the way today's students learn is already here. We must catch up. Flexibility, I've found, is often the single thing, aside from love, that allows students to be successful.

Each student who comes through my door is a hero. I want them to leave superheroes. I want them to conquer the world.

SEPARATING OUT THE GENIUSES

S tudents aren't always recognized for their gifts. Schools value the wrong things.

There is a test score in a box somewhere that says I am a genius. I took the test when I was little. People might not realize I'm a genius when they interact with me, watching me trouble-shoot appliances that aren't plugged in, burn sandwich-shaped outlines in pans, forget stuff, lose keys daily, put fans in closed windows, and show up for important meetings a day early or on Eastern Time when it should have been Pacific. Not "genius" behavior. But the test says so. And so it must be.

There was a kid in my class who solved Rubik's cubes in under a minute but had "F's." I know a guy who can fix anything but doesn't read. Why aren't they "geniuses?" In the zombie apocalypse, they'll recreate life as we know it while I'm still trying to plug in a toaster.

When I was little, we took tests, then they separated the geniuses from the non-geniuses. They assigned the geniuses special classes so we wouldn't become disinterested in school, because if we were bored, there'd be no one to cure cancer.

I learned to feel sad for people who weren't geniuses because they had to do worksheets in "regular" class. I was being "enriched," doing special projects that were much more interesting, designed to tap into my inner creativity. Art, sculpture, writing— that sort of thing.

As Forrest Gump said, "Genius is as genius does." I didn't do much. I'm told I nearly got kicked out of genius class because I always did the bare minimum. While some kids reached for the stars, I asked how many sentences were in a paragraph and wrote just that. Somewhere, there's a book called "My Dad," with four sentences per page. No more. No less. Einstein wouldn't have taken this book from the library.

All the geniuses knew their IQ scores. I wanted to know mine, but my mom wouldn't tell me. She was afraid I'd become a know-it-all like many of the other geniuses. Everyone else's moms made baseball jerseys with theirs and put signs on the front lawn. Finally, I wore Mom down. "It's eighty-four," she said. I was proud. Eighty-four! When people rubbed in their hundred-fifties, I was finally able to share my eighty-four. I was a genius, too!

I found the real score in a file as an adult. It wasn't an eighty-four. It was a number I have no chance of beating. I'm retesting soon—if my students get tested all the time, I should, too. Fair's fair. Truth be told, I'm terrified. The score can only go down. What if I'm no longer a genius, only normal? What then? If it goes down, I guess I'll have to blame my education.

I think about this when I teach. I'm good at tests—we didn't have video games, so I imagined beating the people who made the tests. Even then I knew tests were something to beat, not to learn from. There was a guy in a room rubbing his hands together laughing, "What can we ask her next?" He must be defeated. No different, I suppose, than getting to the next level of a game.

Many kids aren't good at tests. Schools have classes separated by ability level, assigned by tests. This can be a tough thing—it doesn't pull out the real geniuses—the performers. Kids get stuck in "low groups," thinking they aren't smart. If a student is in the "low group" for one class, he or she is usually there for all classes—scheduling's impossible to individualize. In "the low group" students don't stretch their minds toward the stratosphere. They don't reach their potential, because they feel that sense of pity that "these kids can't do that" hearing comments like, "We need someone to serve fast-food." So they become what they hear, feel, and experience, imagining themselves pulling levers for a living rather than innovating solutions. There'll be no curing cancer here.

Ironically, it isn't always the "smart" kid who succeeds in life, but he passes tests and gets the best classes. The kid that succeeds is the kid with enthusiasm and drive who often gets put on the bench—who tries harder because he rebels against the system putting him in a box. "Smart" students are accustomed to the entitlement that accompanies the label, "Oh, I know you meant to do better, you're smart." They get soft, like Rome in its heyday.

I was that person. Good enough was good enough.

Kids take on the identities with which we label them. They should be forging their own. "Genius" and "low group" create students who construct their own glass ceilings out of building blocks we provide with our tests and labels.

Not all kids are great at everything. Be honest and realistic. "I see you're terrible in this, but a genius in that. Learn everything you can. Then follow your passions." Done right, every passion has a job in society—one that makes a living.

"You can't." "Nobody'll pay you to do that." "That's stupid." All my life, I've built boxes around myself. I've had them taped shut. I want my students to break free. I want school to be the road to success.

Schools should be the road, not the roadblock. For every single student.

A score on a piece of paper isn't what motivates students to learn. It's not a predictor of success. It represents weeks where students aren't learning new lessons, months of teachers teaching to the tests, and a bunch of knots in everyone's stomach from the principal on down.

A student's dedication and love of learning is the thing that makes her succeed. A teacher's willingness to teach to the individual is what ignites the passion. The fire spreads.

We have the technology to see what students know at every moment. We can use that same technology to let students shine, using their gifts, pursuing their individual talents and passions.

But I don't think it takes a genius to figure that out.

DO YOU BELIEVE IN ME?

P art of igniting passion in students in making sure they know I believe they're amazing.

I have a question. I need to know the answer. I turn to my students.

"Think of all the teachers you've ever had. No names!" This could get ugly. "I have a question. Do *you* feel *we* believe you will be great? That you'll do amazing things… start companies, innovate, cure diseases, change the world? Do you feel we believe that about you? That you will be an industry leader?"

Pause. Frown. Scrunched up faces... Silence. Then—an explosion. Everyone shouting at once, hands raised, waving around like Italian Sunday dinner.

"No!" "Nobody believes that!" "They think I'm going to be failure." "They told me I wouldn't succeed." "They told me, 'With an attitude like that, what're you gonna do in life?'"

"Wait!" I silence the room. Rioting slows, still simmering—I've created an angry crowd.

"Nobody believes in you? *Nobody*?"

I'm not fishing for compliments. It's just that I spend a great deal of time focusing on motivation. If I'm not succeeding—if they don't feel that I know they'll be great, I'm not great either.

I ask again. They answer. The sad truth is they do not feel every teacher thinks they'll conquer the world. But they report that some do. That's good news, because it only takes one person to steer the ship in another direction. I hope I can do it for each one of them the way it's been done for me, even as an adult. Mentoring, not teaching—it sets up a relationship for life, not just for forty-five minutes for a hundred-eighty days. The thought process changes toward success in life rather than a grade at the end of a course.

I think of the people who believed in me even when I doubted myself. I recall the exact moments. They changed my life forever. I hope these kids have their moments, too. I'd be honored to be one of them.

The steps to "amazing" aren't obvious at seventeen, and "great" isn't always the vision for someone who's been told she's average, or not so smart, for an entire school career. Sometimes kids must overcome substantial life barriers just to arrive at "okay." "Great" ends up being a few miles down the road.

I tell them I give them a lifetime guarantee. If they need help to find their way later in life, find me. I'll be there. That's what all teaching should be. It's a paradigm shift, to be sure.

But today, I look around the room. I tell them they're great again. I say something nice about each one of them, about where I perceive them to be on their journey—a specific talent they should use in their future. The rioting's stopped. There are some smiles. Maybe a few believe they are great now, if just for a moment. Maybe those moments will string together for a day, a week, a month… and before they know it, life itself will be great, too.

28

GREAT TEACHERS LOSE THEIR CLOTHES

Many teachers go to extremes to get kids to learn, including—but not limited to—losing the clothes off their backs.

"Miss, get me those shoes." I'm wearing the black and red Jordan 12's. Anyone in urban education knows what this means. This is social currency, turning me from nerd to cool for a moment. I'm not wearing the right shoes by accident. It's pep rally today. I have to match.

"No."

"I need them for my girlfriend's birthday."

"You don't need them at all. They're overpriced symbols of consumerism made for fifty cents by some kid who wishes he could go to school and wouldn't flunk as much as you."

He doesn't reply. He's trying to process what I just said.

I take pity. I don't need the shoes. I'm just wearing them for theatrics. I play basketball in them and watch students cry. "You'll scuff them!" While they're crying, I score the only basket I'm ever going to get.

"I'll tell you what. Give me a couple bucks and an A. They're yours." Things have no value if they're free.

I know these shoes retail for over $250. I can sell them for more. He knows I know this. He's not outflanking me in negotiation— I have the upper hand. It's supply and demand overlapped by desperation—these shoes are out of stock in stores. It's a good deal. He needs the shoes. I need him to graduate.

He gets his A. I take a hit on the shoes. I wonder if I can get a receipt for tax purposes, declaring the value of the shoes "priceless." That's what his graduation was to me.

I've lost more than shoes. I've given the sweatshirt right off my back on a very cold day. It was baseball season. "Miss, I gotta pitch. It's cold."

"Then you should've brought a sweatshirt." I handed over the hoodie. I froze.

I don't just give my heart and soul teaching. I give pencils, pens, paper and, once in a while, the clothes off my back. That never happened in other jobs. I can't imagine my boss coming up to me and saying, "You got a pen?" Or even, "I have a meeting in fifteen. Can I take your suit jacket?" Yet, in school, this happens quite a bit. We procure items for students, give gift certificates, take collections for kids with serious situations, donate to several scholarship funds and initiatives. We even bring kids school shopping. But a good teacher shouldn't have to give the clothes off his or her back. The role of a teacher is to be involved, care, love, and inspire, not to go broke.

Teachers need to take care of the inspiration and education. Communities must jump in for the rest. The best communities rally around the needs of the schools. The two work hand in hand. When towns create the village it takes to raise a child, everyone's better off, not just the students and families, but the entire community. No one person gives the shirt of his or her back, and citizens work together to give students what they need. In return, they get an entire generation ready to improve life for them.

APPRECIATION

It was parent conference night. The weather was bad and most people stayed home. This meant I could spend as long as I wanted conversing with the families that came, rather than the usual, "Sorry, we only have five minutes. Email me. Next." I like to get to know parents on a personal level. After all, we're all people struggling to get teens to the next level whether they live with us or come late to our class.

One parent stopped me.

"Everyone gives appreciation and gifts to elementary teachers, but nobody appreciates high school teachers," she said. "Before

I go, I wanted to say thank you very much for all that you do."
She handed me a gift card for coffee—my favorite thing in life.
It had a sticky note with apples, saying simply, "Thank you for
all that you do."

I was speechless. In thirteen years of teaching, I've received a
half-dozen cards and a few gifts at the holidays. I can remember them. I never thought about it, but my elementary friends
come out loaded. I don't need gifts. It's not why I teach, but this
simple act of appreciation moved me deeply.

My colleague has students write thank you cards as part of a
class assignment. They pick a teacher or two who influenced
them and write the cards. Some of those have been my most
precious gifts.

"You have changed my life."

"You help me with problems and nobody else takes the time
to listen."

"I really love your antics and the way you teach class."

It makes all the difference. Not the gifts—the appreciation. If
that mom had given me nothing more than the Post-It note with
the thank you message, I'd have felt the same. It makes me remember why I'm here, reminding me to show appreciation every
day to students, colleagues, and family members who entrust

these kids to me, and my own family and friends who put up with my teaching, because a teacher's work, no matter what the pundits say, is never done. It's hard on families. I appreciate that they stand by my calling.

Most of all—and this is the one I often forget—this thoughtful gift reminds me to take a moment and appreciate myself. If I can't do that, it's impossible for me to teach my students to look inward and do the same.

THE LAZARUS TREE

I love trees. There's always something happening—buds, flowers, fiery colors, birds building their homes. Even in winter there's activity while the trees rest, waiting for sap to flow in the spring. Trees are worlds onto their own.

I found an interesting sapling on my school grounds when I started teaching. I'd never seen a tree like it before.

It was on the corner of the wetland leading up to the stairs that for two years smelled like death incarnate. A skunk met its maker. Everyone ran by but no one took action, so we all suffered. The biggest stink happens when people ignore simple problems. It's true for all areas of life.

The tree was about six inches tall, unique—the leaves, the direction of growth. It caught my attention. I watched it grow, and it, I suppose, watched me. We grew together, me in teaching, it in life. Each year we grew a little stronger. My tree and me. My tree became a conscious symbol of passing time.

The tree grew through victories. Students graduated, good years began and ended, seasons passed. The tree grew through difficulties. Students died. Budgets threatened our school, the recession caused my family to struggle. Good and bad years came and went. Still, the tree stood. It remained for better or worse, sickness and health, growing taller. For three years, I looked down on it, soon we stood eye-to-eye. Finally, it towered above me. It's amazing that something can grow so strong in such a short amount of time. I grew strong, too. I felt good about teaching.

A few winters ago a storm got the better of my tree. Ice cracked the main limb. Funny—I was cracking, too. Education was squeezing us all—changing from the joy of serving students to the pressure of measuring the unmeasurable. The tree was warning me, I thought.

But the next year, it sprouted just a bit. I smiled. We all bend under pressure. We survive. My tree made it. So did I.

One day out of nowhere, someone cut it down. Right to the ground.

A tear dropped from my eye to the place where my tree once stood, its growth rings exposed and dying. It was just a tree, I thought, not a life symbol. A tree cannot be a prophet.

It seemed prophetic. It was my worst year yet. I felt like a failure. Cut down, like my tree. Teaching had become data, rubrics, testing, reports… I wasn't good at that stuff. Nothing made sense anymore.

While students were sick with worry about test scores, teachers worried about evaluations and rubric boxes telling us whether we were still worthy to teach. Instantly, I felt a fast-food career in the cards.

"You don't understand," said my friend. "Now they can get rid of bad teachers." I wasn't sure how scaring good teachers helped get rid of bad ones. Bad ones don't care about such things.

Good teachers not only care about students, but bosses, too. They want everyone to smile. The good bosses were smiling less and less under the weight of the world, same as good teachers. The good bosses saw fiscal clouds on the horizon, each connected to numbers they, too, couldn't control. They were getting squeezed even more than good teachers.

"Stop feeling sorry for yourself," said the voice in my head, the one that comes in times of great need. "You've seen this before." It showed me a page from a Soviet history book.

It was about Stalin, gulags, and five-year plans. Soviet dictator Josef Stalin killed millions of his own people in famines and purges. Workers in factories and collective farms were given impossible goals. If they missed their goals, even the ridiculous ones, they'd vacation in Siberia.

The only solution, workers realized, wasn't growth, it was creating the illusion of growth. Predict the lowest numbers possible, then wildly exceed them. Only then would you be a hero.

It's what education was becoming—purges, scapegoatism, and data that no one really used.

I fantasied about leaving education, not because I didn't love teaching, but because I wasn't good at the numbers.

"You're not a teacher, you're a bean counter," said my husband. Being a bean counter wasn't helping my students. It was taking up the time I used to spend preparing good lessons and making me want to die.

I was naive. I'd thought education would be different. The truth is, education is the same as any other field. It's stuck together with the red tape and personal agendas that keep the world on its axis. I'd wanted to escape the evils of the world. Turns out, education is a part of that world.

My idealism died with my tree.

"It's just a tree. There are a thousand trees here. Choose another f'ing tree," said the voice in my head. It was tired of watching me crumble. Education was suffering, I was suffering, my tree was gone.

Never, in a million years, did I think it would go before me. I pictured standing with it the day I retired. I'd pause and think about the world I'd helped change.

Perhaps I couldn't change the world after all...

Every day, I passed the stump. I remembered how things used to be. Would anyone think of me when I was gone? Had I inspired others to grow? Would they pause to remember lessons I taught and pass them on?

Days passed. Weeks. Seasons.

I began to walk by the stump without stopping.

We all get cut down from time to time, pruned back or hacked down. Pruning helps trees grow. Branches spread and provide shade. Same with people—we can grow, or we can die. When we grow, we spread our influence to others.

Truth is, I can't change the world. I can only change me. Then the looming questions answer themselves.

I still felt cut down, but I decided to try—for the sake of my tree, my students, and me—not to let the chainsaw win.

Just the other day I got an email from a former student.

I don't know if you remember me… I did… Thanks for being one of the few teachers who looks forward to going to work in the morning. I hope you inspire the ignorance out of many more students to come!

I think there are more than a few of us. But there are an awful lot of chainsaws, that's for sure.

31

THE WINDMILL

There's a picture of a windmill on my classroom wall over the coffee pot. I look at it while my coffee brews. A Picasso—a silhouette, containing three figures— Don Quixote fighting monsters, contemplating life, and fighting a windmill.

It reminds me every day not to fight windmills. Not to get stuck in red tape—mired, defeated, disillusioned.

Sometimes, I feel like a movie hero tied to railroad tracks, about to get squashed. It's not the students; it's the other things. Simple solutions become, "Let's get a committee on that." Wheel spinning. Giving up. There's always a windmill. A roadblock. An obstacle. Must I fight windmills in order to do the basics?

I found the Picasso of Don Quixote in an art store.

I was Don Quixote—fighting windmills—wearing myself down. A teacher can't fight and teach. It's hard to win a war on two fronts. It's a recipe for burnout—which was coming fast.

There was no denying it. I was Don Quixote, trying to save every Dulcinea that crossed my path.

I bought the Picasso and taped it on my wall. Every morning, I take two or three deep breaths. I look up at the Man of La Mancha. We talk.

"No windmills today, Don Quixote. I promise."

"I'll fight them for you, Dulcinea," he volunteers.

"I'm not Dulcinea. But thank you."

"Dulcinea, there'll be a windmill at 1:30 and another in your mailbox when you leave."

"Thank you, my Don."

I've been warned. Two more breaths. Coffee. A new mantra. "No windmills." If I don't fight the windmills, I can achieve the impossible dream.

THE LOTUS BLOSSOM

I've promised myself I'll no longer fight windmills. Even so, I start to see them everywhere. I'm not sure why. The universe conspires to bring messages I need to hear. It happens when I'm being stubborn—when my good senses refuse to connect with my rational judgment.

First, the universe sends gentle reminders and images. I ignore them. It turns up the volume. I don't listen. Eventually it shouts through a cosmic loudspeaker saying, "Are you really that stupid? Listen up! I mean, I can send a disaster... I'll get your attention..."

It sends windmills... everywhere—in art, literature, on the side of the road. They're fairly common these days. It's not a message... it's easy to ignore. Nothing personal. Just a windmill. The message gets louder and louder. I dismiss it.

Crash!

"Listen up!" says the universe. "Windmills! Stop fighting them!"

I look down at the lance in my hand... the horse at my side. Windmill straight ahead. Guilty look on my face. "Yup," says the lance, "You're about to charge that one now."

Sometimes, when I think I'm affecting change, all I'm really doing is charging windmills.

I met someone who runs around the world doing good things. He doesn't fight windmills—he builds them. He mobilized a group of people to build one in a small village in Kenya. Each person contributed, because not only is it impossible to fight a windmill alone, turns out you can't build one by yourself, either. Today, the windmill stands, bringing water to over six hundred families, stopping regional conflicts over resources. That's making the impossible dream real.

Stop fighting windmills. Build them. Do it together. Change the world—such a powerful lesson. Now, when I stand under my fake Picasso of Don Quixote charging the windmill, I think about using my energy to create, build, flank, and succeed, rather than to smash into obstacles.

Message of the universe noted. I put down the lance.

Lately, I see a lot of lotus flowers. They seem to have the same urgency. "This is the universe speaking, I have a message." I ignore it.

I never thought about lotus flowers before. It was "the frog flower," growing between the lily pads in the murk and mud. We played with frogs and lily pads as children. I grew up near a pond. Sometimes we used the water lilies as targets, trying to hit them with rocks.

I painted a million lotus flowers when I studied Japanese calligraphy and sumi-e painting. I never thought about it though. Ink on rice paper. Flower in the mud. Splotch? Start again.

It's been a while since I've painted a lotus flower. Petals, over and over, ink on rice paper. Painting… breathing… thinking… Until I get it perfect. I never do.

More lotus flowers appear—coincidence? "Hey," says the universe, "I'm talking to you!" I don't listen.

I pass by them when I go running. I find them in books, my login screen, pictures, statues, ponds… I keep seeing them.

"Can you hear us? We're talking to you… pay attention…

You're not listening!" The universe again, speaking louder. "You know, we can send that disaster!"

Still, I pass by. I'm not listening.

It sent the disaster. I got sick—very sick. Sick enough to stop passing the gentle messages the universe sent with a smile. Sick enough to sit in silence for weeks and listen to the messages that were inside me all along. Usually, when I get sick, I push through like a superhero. I fight. I ignore even more. At some point the body breaks down. Then, there is no more fight to be had.

Most people get angry about getting sick during the summer. Being a teacher, it was pretty good timing for me. Almost as if the universe checked my calendar and said, "We've got you penciled in for a good smack. We'll schedule you for after the solstice."

Summer's a good time for recovery… to rest, drink tea, to sit and watch the garden grow into a jungle because I'm not attending to it. To listen to the birds, the peep toads, the sounds of nature. To apologize to the universe, and to myself. To sift through thoughts covered by the clutter of the day-to-day.

To listen.

One day, the lotus spoke again. "You remember me? The flower that grows through the mud?" I did. I said as much. "Have you ever considered my significance? I'm everywhere—art, religion, nature… Have you ever wondered why?"

I confessed I had not. It might as well have been dandelions in art, religion, and nature—they're cool. Resilient things. Can't kill them. I could use one now.

It spoke, "Nothing touches me. I radiate beauty. You can do the same."

"How?" I asked.

"Easy," it said. "I grow in a pond. I take the water and nutrients I need to grow, and let the rest sink to the bottom. What's in mud, anyway? Water, nutrients, life, and a little bit of sludge. Let the sludge go like I do. Then stand tall above the leaves."

I bought a few little lotuses. Jewelry—I never had much jewelry. Some girls seem to attract it. I never did. Now, I wear a little lotus at all times. I want to remember the lesson it taught. Wearing a little lotus is much easier, I think, than carrying around a windmill, and a better message altogether. Instead of simply not fighting obstacles, I picture rising above them, shining. Poking through whatever layers of mud nature sends. Radiating beauty to the world. Being the sun, my favorite star in the sky.

Note to self—send a thank you card to the universe. And to
the lotus.

I started to get better. Summer ended. School began.

A colleague noticed my little lotus.

"That's pretty, but why are you wearing a pot leaf?"

"It's not a pot leaf. It's a lotus flower. The flower that grows
through the mud." He looked. He shrugged. He walked away.

I turned and talked to the new teacher, welcomed her aboard.
She was excited for the start of school, full of joy and ideas. She
made me smile.

"See," said the lotus flower. "Water. Life. Nutrients. When
you settle in, the sediment sinks to the bottom. And you shine
right through."

The universe was right.

I picked up my coffee. Time to get to work.

On becoming a better me.

33

ESCAPING THE CLASSROOM

It seems everyone wants to be a teacher. Once they're in the classroom, they need a path to escape. There is no promotion available for teachers—no career path per se, just steps on a pay scale and thirty years of the same, not counting for policy changes, and land mines to avoid along the way.

"Why are you interested in guidance?" I was speaking with an ex-teacher finishing her guidance certification. She's the type of person I'd want to help my son.

"I'm never going back into the classroom. It's crazy."

"Why?" I asked.

"Because all you do is test. It was getting bad before I started this program, and it's not getting better."

I spoke with another educator. "I think I can escape this nuthouse in a year or two," he said.

"Why?" I inquired. This teacher has always been an inspiration to me.

"This stuff's crazy. I didn't sign on for this. I don't get to do what I love anymore—teach. A robot could do my job."

One person went to administration, saying, "I'll never go back into the classroom," adding, "It's time to move up the ladder."

Time to move up the ladder…

That's something I wonder about. All my expertise doesn't count toward "moving up." I can get eight PhDs and still be "just a teacher." Not one step up "the ladder." The extra degrees are actually a liability. School districts have to pay more for teachers with advanced degrees.

A colleague summed this up nicely. "Casey, you're a tenth-step teacher with a masters. If someone tells you your job is to balance on a circus ball, then that's what you do!" I wouldn't be hired by anyone else—I was simply too expensive. If I didn't stay in one place forever, I'd have to leave the field.

There's no room for teachers to "move up," even as we seek to improve ourselves. We can stay put or we can move out of the classroom. Moving out is sad, because it forces us to forsake the reason we came in the first place—the kids.

If education is truly about lifelong learning, there needs to be a pathway to keep expert teachers teaching without the perception it's the bottom rung and everything outside of the classroom is a promotion.

Everybody needs growth. We need educational leaders that will change the world just as much as we need teachers who do. Teachers should strive to be educational leaders because they have something to offer. No teacher, however, should feel he or she must leave the classroom because there's nowhere left to go.

I saw a teacher packing boxes, departing mid-year. Most of his stuff was already gone. "Teaching's crazy. All I do is test, fill in rubrics, and prepare for observations and evaluations. It's not what I thought. It's not for me."

"If it makes you feel any better," I said, "maybe it is for you... I've been teaching a while, and this particular year, with all the changes, I'm wondering the same thing. It's not you at all."

"I'm not interested in this. I can make a bigger impact in education outside the classroom."

Someone said the same thing to me a couple years ago.

I was talking about the windmills, how I was frustrated. How education was changing in a direction that disturbed me.

"Have you ever stopped to think," my friend said, "you might be spinning your wheels? That you can have a much bigger effect on education *outside* the classroom? Don't answer now. Just think about it," he said.

I've been thinking about it ever since.

The classroom is supposed to be the central focus of education— everything else supporting that mission. Lately it feels like it's flipped upside down. It's hard to improve education with the best and the brightest leaving the field.

The normal trickle of farewell has turned into a mass Exodus where people outsprint Moses and the Israelites across the Red Sea to get out of teaching. It's not healthy or good for the students. Students need teams that treat them like the rock stars they are rather than test numbers on a spreadsheet. It's tough to create that climate with people constantly saying goodbye.

"If teaching is so great, then why does everyone always want to get out of the classroom?"

That's the million-dollar question.

Sometimes a very special person gets it right, "I didn't want

to leave the classroom, but I think I can help students more
in this way."

That's the kind of leadership that affects change. Those are the
people who change the world.

35

WORKING TOGETHER

The world gets cranky when the issue of public education comes up in conversation. They say we're not producing the kind of employees anyone wants anymore—we're disconnected from reality and it shows in the graduates we impose on them.

"Send me people I can use! That don't want to go home at five o'clock and get paid a hundred grand for the honor!" My friend knew I wasn't the single educator responsible for his subpar employee, just a representative of teachers at large.

"I'm trying…" I get bitched at a lot. I listen to stories of millen-

nial entitlement and lazy employees as if I, personally, created
the conditions where young adults can't add or tell time without
iPhones. Education's had two complete philosophical shifts since
I've been alive. The teachers who survived the neon sixties taught
me to feel, create, do. I learned to think outside the box. Then the
"test, memorize, evaluate," high-stakes swing of the pendulum
came back into play. That's how I'm supposed to teach.

Students who had "multiple opportunities for success" all
throughout their schooling now they expect it from their bosses.
Bosses are not amused. That's why they get mad at me.

"Education reform's not working, maybe you should try something else," I'm told as if I have the power.

Education reform hasn't been smooth, that's for sure. I like
cars. I think education reform should be more like driving a
Maserati than driving a Vespa over potholes. I'm imagining
driving the Maserati, of course. I've never seen a teacher drive
a Maserati. We all have economical cars or clunkers, like my
faithful Forester Gump.

I imagine driving a Maserati would be smooth—clean and sleek,
upshifting, downshifting, changing direction at the first site of
an obstacle in the road. The obstacle's probably the muffler my
car left behind. If I had the power, education reform would be
smooth like driving the sports car. Not only would the bosses
like my friends be happy, but the students would be as well.
After all, I'm not producing products for sale on a shelf. I'm

175

serving living, breathing kids, who have opinions and thoughts about how they'd like to spend life—valid thoughts, hopes, dreams, and aspirations.

I try to tell students how to avoid pissing off bosses and how to love their jobs.

As the representative of all educators everywhere, I'm sorry my boss-friend is mad. American education cannot be fixed by policy changes alone. It's silly to think we live in a vacuum where testing, tweaking, writing new standards, then testing some more can solve the ills of society. There will always be something to improve.

Our solution isn't to think outside the box, it's to open the box wide and let others in.

This nation has always produced the best and the brightest innovators in the world. To fix our problems, we need to bring them to the table. We need to include everyone in the tough conversations. No one succeeds in life alone. Education can't either.

I'm inviting my boss-friend to the table. He's a decent entrepreneur. Entrepreneurs innovate and reinvent society. Education needs that right now. More importantly, entrepreneurs hire my students. They deserve a voice, too. Right now, many of them are rattling sabers saying, "Education's broken! Homeschool! Boycott! Break it apart and reconstruct. Revolt!"

I'd tell them to use the sabers, instead, to cut through the jungle that's tangling my feet and the red tape binding my hands.

After I invite my friend to the table, I'm going to invite students. If teachers are treated like the "little guy" in education, students are powerless, voiceless, nowhere to be seen. After all, every change we make in education reform is "for the students." They need a voice in crafting the solutions.

If we bring everyone to the table, all the different thoughts, we'll have a good shot at success. We've got no chance on our own. We'll simply do a whole lot of preaching to the choir.

Together, we're much greater than the sum of our parts. Together, we're magic.

T he world of education and the world of entrepreneurship are very different spaces. They have incredibly different processes, ideologies, and standard operating procedures. I started out "just a teacher" but wandered cluelessly into a circle of amazing innovators.

I loved watching people create things out of thin air—products, jobs, services that helped the universe. One day, it dawned on me—that's the real world.

Is school preparing my students for the real world? Can they go out, take charge, and lead the next generation of great? Did my cranky friend have a point?

The two worlds, education and entrepreneurship... education and real life... need to be one and the same. Today's education system was designed during the industrial revolution. It's stagnant. The world of business and entrepreneurship is live and vibrant. If one of the two must change, it's probably education.

I was watching a video of a talk featuring Kleiner Perkins Caufield & Byers' venture capitalist Dana Mead. Mr. Mead spoke to a room full of Stanford students learning venture capital as a career. Educators don't generally listen to venture capitalists speak, but as I listened, something in me liked the idea very much—investing other people's money rather than getting a second job to pay for my classroom. It sounded attractive. I paid attention.

He was telling a story about entrepreneurship. He said East Coast and West Coast entrepreneurs are very different—neither is better or worse, they're just different. An entrepreneur on the East Coast who said, "I've been in three failed ventures, I'm starting number four," might get some resistance and negative reactions. West Coast entrepreneurs got handshakes and a slew of, "Congratulations, I know number four's going to be great!"

The West Coast climate, it seems, recognizes starting a new

venture is difficult. People learn along the way. Anyone who's worked with three or four companies or startups—regardless of their success—has a wealth of information. They're crafting their skill. A high level of encouragement, even in the face of failure, is critical.

Mr. Byers noted the tendency of West Coast entrepreneurs to reach out to people for no other reason but to assist. They'd been through it before and were in a position to help others avoid pitfalls. Being an entrepreneur is hard. Failure doesn't always mean failure. It means learning. Sometimes it takes practice to get it right. It always takes help.

Education needs to be more like West Coast entrepreneurship. We've become paralyzed—failure is so high-stakes we're afraid to try new things.

"I can't do that," teachers say. "It might affect my numbers." Everyone sticks with what they know because it worked in the past. We fear falling short. We want to be left alone to our numbers so we don't get fired or hurt our students' test scores.

Education's not alone. Entrepreneurs measure things. They have goals, too. There are market factors even the best analyst couldn't predict. Sometimes the world implodes despite the best intentions of the founders or the team, and the numbers go south.

The best and the brightest get up, dust off, and try again. Education needs to create an environment where this is possible, encouraged, even congratulated. Where we take failure—not that we want one, mind you—but we take it and say, "How can we improve?"

Just because a student failed or a teacher's data doesn't reach a stated goal doesn't label him a failure. It could mean any number of things. The key is staring down the situation and fixing it—using the West Coast mentality.

Education must acknowledge there are factors out there that dwarf even the greatest teacher or principal, and sometimes things don't turn out the way we plan. In today's climate, that's career ending. Students don't graduate, teachers leave the field, and principals are replaced so schools can be "transformed."

Success isn't measured in one lesson or one test. It's long-term. Lifelong.

Time to practice the lessons we preach. When we shift the paradigm from one that measures human capital as if it were mass-produced to one that looks into the hearts and souls of those we serve, we'll have it right.

Educators can't do this alone. When someone says, "How can I help?" we need to accept that help.

I see that now, quite by accident, because a student wanting to use technology in school embarrassed me one day by asking, "Why not?" and I failed to provide an answer. That failure forced me to search for better answers than "Because there's a rule."

I found there was a whole world out there where people were asking the same questions, where people turned failures and "whys" into successes and "why nots."

PUT AWAY THE PHONE

Schools aren't always the centers of innovation that they should be.

"You have to put away your phone." That's what I was supposed to say. My student was using his phone to take notes. He was a top-level student, technically with "special needs," who didn't write well with a pencil. He had apps, pictures, note pads, and productivity tools. He used them efficiently like the best CEO, scheduling, arranging, writing, and sending right from the phone. I was impressed. I was also light years behind. I had no idea about the power of technology in the classroom.

He wanted to use his phone. I wanted to let him.

Still, there was a rule. A rule on a bright, blinking neon sign. "No Phones Allowed." I asked why. No one could give me a real answer. Someone said it might cause a ripple in the time-space continuum. Others said "They might record you without your knowledge."

I had a vision of students recording me without my knowledge then going home and listening to my class over and over and over. Learning? Sounded pretty good to me.

We didn't have class computers then, and the library was usually full or closed. There was a computer lab, but it had old, bulky monitors whose screens flickered. I think the late 1980s eventually sent a truck to pick them up. I didn't like to go to the computer lab, anyway, because if I did go, I'd lose ten minutes bringing students down, have to hunt for kids who "forgot" we were meeting there, and the kid who needed more time the next day was out of luck. It was a pain.

Why couldn't I just let them use phones?

"It's the rule." The Rule. Educators must obey and enforce The Rules. It's what we do. It's in our code of ethics.

My students had phones more powerful than my first computer. It seemed like a rule meant to be broken—or, as Carmen Medina would've said—changed.

My student pressed the issue. I was embarrassed. He was right and I was powerless. I should be the one leading the charge. I was the adult.

I set out on a quest to find solutions. My students were born in the digital age. Schools were not. I, a dinosaur, imagined a school where students used their smartphones to calendar in homework reminders or take pictures of notes on the board. It was my entire vision for technology at the time. I decided it was time for me to research better ways to get the job done. I was in for a shock.

My entire plan was this: I figured I'd ask my computer friends if they knew any teachers who had computers without classroom budgets, or schools who let students use cellphones to take pictures of notes on the board. Then, I'd figure out how to bring that information back home.

Not all computer people are created equal, however. Many don't know a thing about education. It turns out education technology is a specialty. "Sorry." "No." "I don't know anything about education," said every computer friend I asked.

One day, I grumbled to an old college friend with whom I reconnected.

"There's a lot going on in edtech, I'd be happy to introduce you to someone in that vertical," said my friend, a writer, who confessed he was really a "startup guy."

"Startup what?" There needs to be a noun at the end of that sentence. *You have to start something,* I thought. He said he did, tech companies. He didn't deal with education. He didn't even like education. He said it was too messed up to fix. He was offering to introduce me to someone who thought education could be saved—a person who knew my world.

In the tech world, introductions are big things. Formal, even. People are busy, and no one gets through the gatekeepers without introductions. I had no idea about such things—a teacher chained to a desk doesn't receive introductions.

I was excited, expecting my friend would introduce me to some broke teachers with no computers who let their kids use smartphones to take pictures of the board or calendar in homework assignments. Then, in accordance with the plan, it'd be my job to figure out how they got their schools to say yes.

He never did introduce me to broke teachers. Instead, he led me to a world of technology, innovation, discovery. The matrix. Once I entered the matrix, the world was never the same. I took the red pill, fell down the rabbit hole, met some of the greatest minds in the universe. Each was more inspirational than the last. They solved problems. Quickly.

They didn't need an act of Congress to move a copy machine or a committee to act on an idea. They just did things. In education, having an idea gets a person in trouble—it gets you put on three committees where the idea eventually dies in session or receives a pocket veto.

I was entering a whole new world—a world where failure wasn't a career ender; it was a step on the road to success.

And it was true. People actually said, "I know you will be great. How can I help you?"

This paradigm shift is the missing ingredient in education—the game changer. The solution. The thing that can get teachers out of their boxes taking chances again. Failure wouldn't be irreversible. Learning from difficulties would signify the mastering of a craft.

I had felt disenfranchised, powerless, institutionalized. Suddenly, everything was different. Renewed. Possible. My epiphany—*reform needed to be reformed.* There were people out there trying to do it. I started to pay very close attention to what the entrepreneurs had to say. More importantly, I realized I could make a difference, too—I was no different than anyone else on the journey. I learned we're all just people walking the walk, taking one step at a time, each navigating our own minefields as we do.

The difference—the successful people don't stop at that single step. They learn to walk around the land mines. If one blows up and leaves them standing, they push by the fear and take another step. That is the entire secret.

A journey of a thousand miles doesn't start with one single step. It starts with the intent to take a step. It continues with the actual step, and it succeeds somewhere down the line. Lifting just one foot brings the power to change the world.

And so I resolved to take my first step.

Then I did.

FREE TICKETS

I was lucky enough to hear entrepreneurial rock star Steve Blank speak at the Business Innovation Factory conference in Providence last year, and I've paid attention to his message ever since. Mr. Blank has done it all—founded, sold, and advised several companies and invested in a bunch more. He teaches some of the nation's top entrepreneurs at Stanford, and has gone so far as to help sectors of the federal government learn to spend money wisely. That's no small achievement. He told a story.

He said he's seen a lot of startups in his career. He always knew a company was doing badly when he went to a meeting and saw a new Vice-President of Sales—as if the old one just evaporated, and there, in front of him, was a new one sitting in the chair.

"That last idea was clearly a bad one," the new VP would say. "We're going to do it this way now." Everything changed, people were purged, and the cycle continued.

"What if," Mr. Blank went on to say, "we fired *the idea,* not *the person?"*

"That changes everything," he said. People would take chances again. They'd think outside the box. They would go for the gold. They wouldn't always duck and cover.

Education breeds a great deal of scapegoatism and fear. Education can't be like a Soviet five-year plan where people are fabricating data trying to escape the next purge. People need to have the confidence to collaborate, speak the truth, identify areas of opportunity, and fix them.

If, like Mr. Blank said, education had the courage to "fire the idea," instead of the person, people would solve problems. They wouldn't hide. They'd collect real numbers instead of the ones needed to secure funding or save their jobs. They'd ask the tough questions, and see where the true areas of opportunity lie. Nobody would blame teachers, students, parents, or policy so much. We'd eat dinner at the same table like the family we are. We'd get the job done.

"Fire the idea." This way of thinking creates a safe zone where people will throw their best out there, even if they seem impossible. The best ideas come from outside the echo chamber and way outside the box—that's where the vision lies. That's where "impossible" becomes every day.

When people operate out of fear, they cling to a safety zone that keeps them from reaching for greatness.

Vision is the opposite of fear. Vision is the ability to look uncertainty in the eye and say, "I'm giving this my all." That's the type of permission teachers and educational leaders need—they need to build a system that supports and rewards visionary thinking.

Sometimes ideas and policies aren't good. It takes a big person to say that. "Fire the idea." Rally the team. Create an environment that doesn't reach for the stars—it discovers them.

It's what I want for every school in the universe.

39

YOU DIE, I DIE, WE BOTH DIE

Many of today's problems—in and out of education—can be solved studying Eastern philosophy.

I spent years studying Japanese swordsmanship. It's less about killing people these days and more about studying the laws of the universe—quite Zen.

There's something about large bladed weapons that interests my students even if I never defeated anyone in Tokugawa Japan or reached enlightenment. They all want to see a demonstration of me hacking something or someone to pieces.

If I could bring swords to school, which I fear would bring more

Homeland Security to my demonstration than students, they'd
be disappointed. They'd see a demo of me sitting in silence,
meditating, with a couple of sword slashes interrupting the wait.
It's not what most people expect.

Still, I talk swords with them from time to time. As far as cutting
down real people, I admit I sliced my left foot once while practicing—I have a small battle scar. I tell them I've been smashed
around a lot and hit over the head with wooden objects—they
can tell their parents that explains their grades. My students
relish the vision of me being smacked and tossed around. But
there's a story I tell that means something to me and is important
for both of us. They listen.

"When swordsmen fight a dual," I say, "there are only three outcomes. You die, I die, or we both die." I ask a question, "What
are the mathematical chances of dying in a sword fight?" They
always get it wrong.

"Fifty-percent." Makes sense. There are two people fighting.
One hundred percent divided by two. They're mad I've brought
math into the conversation.

"You're wrong." I tell them we need more math in schools. I
give them a hint. "You die, I die, or we both die." They recalcu-
late. They come up with fifty-percent again. There are still two
people fighting.

195

"The answer," I say, "is sixty-six percent."

They're puzzled. They run the math in their minds.

I explain.

"Well, we're both standing here with swords." I put a kid in front of me for effect. For the tiniest fraction of a second, he looks at my empty hands as if I might cut him in two pieces. Then he won't have to take my test.

"Three things can happen. First, I cut you, you die. Second, you cut me, I die. But since we're both very skilled, most likely the two swords come out so fast we both cut each other instantly. It takes a couple minutes for us both to bleed to death while we stare each other down. We both die. Three outcomes. Thirty-three percent chance I live. But sixty-seven percent chance I die."

Unless… there's no fight.

I tell them the story of "the sword of no sword." It's the story of master swordsman Yamaoka Tesshu as recounted in John Stevens' "The Sword of No Sword."

When a swordsman reaches a certain level, everyone issues a challenge. It's like being the big guy on the block. Everyone wants to kick your behind and be the next Big Guy. This is a lose-lose proposition for the Big Guy. There's no glory in beating someone inferior—what football player punches a kindergartener? The only sure victory is not to fight.

The story says Master Tesshu was repeatedly challenged to duals by young and upcoming samurai. One in particular wouldn't leave him alone. Master Tesshu finally accepted the challenge, on one condition—the fight would occur on a small island away from the public. The challenger agreed, and they rowed out to the island.

"I forgot my sword," said Master Tesshu. Master Tesshu instructed the swordsman to prepare for the dual while he went back for his sword. He rowed away from the island and never returned—victory without fighting. Master Tesshu had nothing to prove.

When I constantly fight and resist, that's the ego shining through. Winning in that way never gets me closer to my goals. It just gets me tired.

I've spent most of my career being the little guy fighting and crusading senselessly with no end result—so many good causes left unresolved. Windmills. Red tape. Road blocks. Bureaucracy—there's always a Goliath to fight. I could spend my entire life fighting the good fight with no results. That's just silly.

Master Tesshu's lesson shows by avoiding one fight at a time, any problem, insurmountable as it may seem, can be solved. "The sword of no sword," is the secret to sanity in education. Let go of the fight. Just be. If enough people realize this, we'll all be sane together.

When I'm the little guy challenging the big guy all the time, I get left on the island. Every time.

What if I flipped the equation? What if, instead, I was Master Tesshu leaving the other guy on the island? Leaving behind the red tape, bureaucracy, the things that seem to get in the way? If I leave them on island, one by one, each and every nonproductive thing, I win in the end. I get peace. My kids learn life lessons, not only class material.

"The sword of no sword." Fighting without fighting. Leaving ego far, far behind.

If I choose to fight, there's only a thirty-three percent chance of walking out alive. By not fighting, my chances increase to one hundred percent. Those are odds I'll play in Vegas every time.

WHAT NOW?

Take these stories. Laugh. Read. Relate. Perhaps one or two are you. Maybe you've felt the same way, you've struggled—tried to do the best you could. You've wondered, at times, if you'd have the energy to stay in education. I hope you do. I hope you realize the immense power you hold in your hand, the impact you make, the lives you change.

I knew I couldn't write a book about how to teach, and anyway, there are enough of those out there on every nuance of pedagogy. They'll give you step-by-step instructions for everything under the sun. I can only write a book about my experience. I write about how the lessons of the classroom instead teach me.

I'd like to state definitively how to fix public education—how to get rid of high-stakes testing and evaluations, how to show the world that my students are amazing. I can't do that either. I'd be fighting windmills again, and I promised to stop. I've realized something...

I cannot change the world.

I can only change me.

In changing me, I've found I've had far more impact than I ever would've imagined back when I was fighting windmills and dunking horses' heads in water to make them drink. Simply serving students, genuinely caring about them, and having love and respect for their ideas rather than simply handing them the official cannon teaches me more about myself. We become great together. That's how the world—and the universe—gets changed.

Teaching is a subtle process of self-discovery—the opposite of instant world changing. We treat learning like the running of the bulls when, in fact, it's quiet, more like the whisper of the slightest breeze or the flapping wings of a butterfly. The true moments of impact are seldom heard. They are no louder than the growing of a blade of grass, the lotus flower popping silently through the mud, or the ripple of a small stream eventually flowing into a raging river, then dumping into the ocean. I am the small stream. The ocean never comes until much, much later. True teaching is that subtle.

This book was born out of a promise to a friend. In keeping that promise, I ask others to keep promises to me. They, in turn, extract promises from others.

And so it continues and continues, until the stream flows into the ocean, and the stars shine bright over every corner of the land. That is how true change is sustained.

DEDICATION

I teach because I was taught. Great teachers touched my life. They molded and shaped me. They did subtle things, things I didn't understand until years later. They were direct, pointed, and real. I remember them. Not all remember me.

I'd visit and say, "Look, I'm teaching! Because of you!" Some were ecstatic. Others, disinterested. One gave me a blank stare. "Who are you?" Someone called me by my sister's name.

This book holds the spirit of the under-recognized teachers who shaped me.

Mrs. Stanulonis, Mrs. Shores, Mr. Juhl, Mr. Herden, Brother Norris, Mr. Lander, Mr. Kessler and Mr. Brown—the unheralded high school instructors who shaped my life, thank you. You taught me to type, write, analyze, love learning, mentor, and provide a lifetime guarantee to my students. I couldn't have had a better principal than Mr. Warren.

As an undergrad, Dan Harrison let me fail out of music with grace, but Alvin Parris and Paul Burgett taught me music was for everyone, that passion is the key element, not only in music, but in life.

Stephen Hutchings gave me a love for great literature. I hope he's forgiven me for not fully appreciating his lessons until graduate school. He is the professor who called me when I skipped class. Doug Brooks implored me to study things off the beaten path. That changed my life. Brenda Meehan was one of those few people I've met who was truly holy. She was an exemplar for how I treat my students.

Stan Lemons gave me the honor of proofreading chapters of his book *First Baptist Church of Rhode Island.* It is the greatest privilege for a graduate student to touch the work of such a scholar. He was responsible for "the good example of a bad book."

Ron Dufour and Larry Hudson taught me all I needed to know about historiography. This translated to the ability to see everything through multiple lenses, a critical skill I teach today. Bob Cvornyek proved a real writer and historian can write about anything. The story is in all of us. He showed me great people are simply ordinary folks who never stop working hard.

Each one of these people taught a different lesson. I use these lessons every day.

It turns out, I am a little bit of each one every time I open my classroom door.

I'm ever so grateful.

THANK YOU

T hank you for reading this book and coming with me on my journey. I'm honored.

I never expected to write this book. It was a promise to Kamal Ravikant and Claudia and James Altucher. Kamal insisted I write "for real." James says everyone has a book in him, but Claudia had enough love to reject my first project, which would've been awful.

"That's not your story right now," she said. "You should write about teaching. I'd want to read that." I wasn't so sure. Claudia was right.

I didn't want to kill another tree in the name of public education. I simply wanted to show my journey. A lot of good people are getting lost in the shuffle of education reform. I wanted anyone with a voice—and especially the voiceless—in education walk a few steps beside me through the side effects of reform. I hope these stories help people think about how well-intentioned reform filters downstream. That was the story I set out to write—the one

I hope Claudia wanted to read.

Keeping my promise to write "for real," made me a better teacher and person. Thank you.

I'm a long way from my Pulitzer, I have more gratitude. Sarah Steenland and Berni Xiong gave me to the green light in the first-draft "yes or no" stage. Jason Croft and Kathleen Jasper, both passionate about education, pulled apart this work and made me dig deeper. Kathleen told me to stop pulling punches. Teachers are trained to be polite and politically correct. Sometimes that doesn't get the job done.

Thanks to the Learnist crew—my first experience in edtech before I knew the word existed. You've been life changers for me, especially Crystal, Farb, David, Christian, and Aaron.

Marianne Dombroski kept me sane, and Heather Gilchrist pulled me off some cliffs in business, education, and life.

Jodi Swanson's "What ifs" kept me laughing and thinking in the right direction. She is the supermodel on the cover. When I said I didn't know what to do about the book cover, "unless Jesus floats down from heaven and hands me one," Erin Tyler, the best designer in the world, suddenly appeared. I always knew God was female.

Finally, thanks to my whole family, especially my husband

Rusty, who survived my teaching, writing, and general chaos, my sister Mary who read the first edit of this manuscript, and my sister-in-law Ali, who contributed the author photograph.

Most of all, thank you to my students. You are amazing, and will conquer the world. All you need to do is take one step forward. Then, keep walking.

ABOUT DAWN CASEY-ROWE

I'm a teacher, writer, nerd, runner, earth-loving, sustainability-driven vegetarian, business owner, and scatterbrain. I am a non-linear thinker, a 5 a.m. riser, 10 p.m. sleeper. I drink too much coffee.

I want to inspire near and young adults to be amazing, so they'll return with gratitude for life in their hearts and money in their pockets. I want them to live lives that make the world better while they smile every day.

I love mason jars and growing the foods I eat. I hope to rid the world of processed foods, one box and carton at a time.

Sometimes, I pause to write about the important things, even if it gets me bad karma. I'm trying to raise a boy who will add love to the universe.

Most of all, I want world peace and an end to human suffering. And another cup of coffee.

You can find me at my blog, CafeCasey.com, on Twitter at @runningdmc, writing about education on the web, or connect with me by email at dawn@cafecasey.com. I'm grateful you shared this time with me.